Kitchen
Gardening
for beginners

Kitchen Gardening
for beginners

Simon Akeroyd

DK

LONDON, NEW YORK, MUNICH,
MELBOURNE, DELHI

Project Editors May Corfield,
Hilary Mandleberg
Senior Art Editor Alison Gardner
Senior Editor Chauney Dunford
Photography Peter Anderson
Projects Alexander Storch
Jacket Designer Rosie Levine
Senior Producer Seyhan Esen
Producer, pre-production George Nimmo
Picture Research Susie Peachey
Managing Editor Penny Warren
Managing Art Editor Alison Donovan
Publisher Mary Ling
Art Director Jane Bull

DK Publishing
North American Consultant Kate Johnsen
Senior Editor Rebecca Warren

First American Edition, 2013
Published in the United States by DK Publishing,
375 Hudson Street, New York, New York 10014
13 14 15 16 17 10 9 8 7 6 5 4 3 2 1
001—187261—Apr/2013
Copyright © 2013 Dorling Kindersley Limited
All rights reserved

Published in Great Britain by
Dorling Kindersley Limited.
A catalog record for this book is available from
the Library of Congress.
ISBN 978-1-4654-0961-4
Printed and bound by
South China Co. Ltd China.
Discover more at **www.dk.com**

Contents

Simon Akeroyd was brought up in a family of professional cooks, but discovered from an early age that he preferred growing food to cooking it. He has written for numerous gardening magazines, including the monthly Allotment Gardener pages for *Grow Your Own* magazine. He was previously a Garden Manager for the Royal Horticultural Society, and has worked at both RHS Wisley and RHS Harlow Carr. He also worked for the BBC as a horticultural researcher and producer. He has an allotment in Surrey and is an avid beekeeper. His previous books include *Shrubs and Small Trees, Lawns and Ground Cover, The RHS Allotment Handbook,* and *Grow Your Own Fruit.*

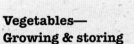

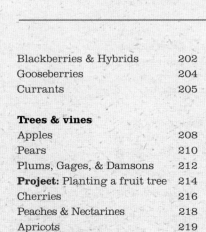
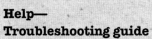

Introduction

The popularity of kitchen gardens has increased enormously over the last few years, which is no surprise. Many of us live hectic desk-bound lifestyles and eat supermarket produce. We crave open spaces and homegrown fruit and vegetables—not to mention a little exercise. Working in the garden answers all these needs. Give it a try and you'll never look back.

Reaping the benefits

Growing your own food gets you outdoors and into the fresh air but it also brings many other benefits and rewards.

◆ **KITCHEN GARDENERS** eat more healthily than many. Having grown the recommended five-a-day portions of fruit and vegetables, they will not want to let them go to waste.

◆ **WORKING IN** the garden provides a fantastic outdoor workout; your muscles will ache but only in a good way.

◆ **RELAX YOUR MIND** while you garden. Leave your worries behind as you concentrate on your plants.

◆ **YOUR GARDENING** expertise will increase along with the range of fruit and vegetables you grow.

◆ **ENJOY SAVING MONEY** while you work. You are bound to appreciate harvesting tasty, fresh produce for the cost of only a few packets of seeds.

Tools

Every gardener needs decent tools to do the job. Don't rush to the nearest garden center though; you can often buy secondhand tools via online ads or at auctions or yard sales. Choose tools that suit your height and build, and be sure they feel comfortable and balanced to hold. Look after them well and clean them after use, then they will last a lifetime. The list of basic tools to get you started includes:

- a spade
- a fork
- a landscape rake
- a dibber
- garden twine or string
- a trowel
- a hand fork
- a long-handled cultivator
- Dutch and draw hoes
- a watering can
- a wheelbarrow
- edging shears
- a mower (for grass paths)

Having the right tools for the job makes working in the garden considerably easier.

Old to new

Gardens pass from homeowner to homeowner. Hopefully, when you purchase your home there will be elements in your yard that you would be wise to retain. Old fruit bushes and trees can be revived; dilapidated raised beds and overgrown paths can be restored. Think renovation instead of demolition.

Established plants will prove to be a blessing when you are just starting out.

Wooden pallets dumped on the plot can be transformed into a compost bin.

Patio slabs left lying around can be used for paths or even seating areas.

Making friends

Whether you are retired, want to grow enough to feed your family, or just love feeling the soil between your fingers, the gardening life can be truly fulfilling. You may already be an experienced gardener, but if you have recently moved and are working in a new yard, you may encounter new gardening challenges. New homes mean new neighbors, and they may have expertise in dealing with the same issues that you are facing. Many of these gardeners will be only too pleased to offer help and advice, some of which will have come from their years of experience. It is like having your very own panel of gardening experts. Watch for opportunities and welcome them with drinks or tasty treats, perhaps some that were grown in your own garden.

Gardening is a great way of spending quality time with the family. Not only do children enjoy gardening, but it gets them away from computers and TV screens and out in the fresh air.

Bring a cold drink out to your yard and enjoy a well-earned break with neighbors.

YARD ETIQUETTE
- Try to greet your neighbors and introduce yourself.
- Keep the boundaries that surround your yard clear.
- Don't allow weeds from your yard to go to seed and spread.
- Don't erect things or do any planting that will cast shade on others' yards.
- Take care if using chemicals.

Garden plot sizes

Kitchen gardens vary according to the space available in your yard and your interest in growing a variety of produce. These days, sizes of plots vary enormously and there are no hard-and-fast rules. If you are just starting out, it is better to start small; a full-sized plot can be daunting and will often involve considerably more maintenance than you may have expected. If you don't feel confident taking on a large garden on your own, consider asking a friend to help share in the cost and maintenance. Both of your families can then benefit from the fruits of your labors.

Reuse and recycle

When you begin to garden, you will quickly discover how to become a master of recycling. You won't let anything go to waste.

◆ **HANG OLD CD**s among your crops and they will act as bird scarers; empty toilet paper rolls miraculously become seed starters; and old tires filled with soil prove perfect for growing potatoes.

◆ **REUSE PLASTIC POTS** and flats; you can never have enough at seed-sowing time.

◆ **PLASTIC BOTTLES** make cloches for protecting young seedlings. Pushed into the soil and filled with water, they become handy reservoirs.

About this book

The first three chapters of this book show the progression of a newly acquired garden, from planning and preparation, to the well-earned harvest. These chapters also feature step-by-step projects, built and photographed in a real garden, to show what can be achieved in the first year. The final chapter explains how to troubleshoot problems, while a useful glossary will help you understand unfamiliar gardening terminology.

Real garden Watch the development of a real plot over the course of a year.

Practical help Advice panels help get the best from even difficult sites.

10 steps to preparing your plot Starting with a new garden, follow the steps in sequence to ensure success. Take time to assess and plan your site properly before starting work, to avoid problems later on.

Raised beds Follow the step-by-step guide to make your own.

Materials needed Use these guides as a shopping list, so you have everything you need at every stage.

Projects You don't have to be an expert at DIY to follow these straightforward guides to making features for your plot. All projects involve simple tools and materials that are widely available.

Additional info boxes These provide useful tips to make tasks easier, or suggest other options.

Chapter 1:
Preparing the plot

This chapter explains the 10 essential steps required to bring a new garden to life. Starting with assessing the site to decide what crops will grow best, it shows how to prepare the soil, sow seeds under cover or outside, then illustrates all the tasks and techniques necessary for a bumper crop. The chapter also features simple step-by-step projects to help make the most of the site. These include laying paths and making raised beds, erecting rabbit-proof fencing, and making a cold frame. This chapter also reminds you to enjoy your plot, and to take time to make it your own.

Chapters 2 & 3:
Growing vegetables & fruit

These chapters provide in-depth growing instructions to over 70 different fruits, vegetables, and herbs. Starting with sowing seeds or planting new plants, the instructions cover every stage of each crop's development, explaining what to do, when, and how. There are also step-by-step projects, showing how to build features that make growing your crops easier and more successful.

Storing & Using

After the excitement of growing your food comes the joy of eating it. Every grower is thrilled to have a bumper crop but what to do when you are faced with extras?

Storing Discover how best to store your crops so that they can be enjoyed in perfect condition.

Freezing You can extend the life of much of your produce by freezing it; discover how to do it and how long it can be stored.

Cooking There are lots of exciting recipe ideas to help you make the most of your crops.

Preserving Delicious jams, preserves, and chutneys can be made from extra fruits and vegetables.

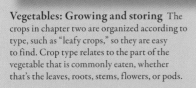

Info boxes Refer to the panels for timely tips and advice.

Vegetables: Growing and storing The crops in chapter two are organized according to type, such as "leafy crops," so they are easy to find. Crop type relates to the part of the vegetable that is commonly eaten, whether that's the leaves, roots, stems, flowers, or pods.

Fruit: Growing & storing The fruit crops featured in chapter three are either soft fruits, such as strawberries and raspberries, or tree and vine fruits, such as apples and grapes,

Chapter 4: Help

This final chapter shows how to prevent or resolve many of the common problems that can occur in gardens. Illustrated galleries help to identify pests, diseases, and weeds, and give advice on how to treat them. There is also practical advice on pruning fruit trees and bushes to keep them healthy, and a guide to propagating your own plants when you need to increase your stocks.

steps **1-10**
to preparing your plot

step 1

assessing your site

an established site • garden checklist • carrying out renovations • an overgrown site • sunny & shady sites

step 1 Assessing your site

Your first day in your new garden site may seem daunting, particularly if it has become very overgrown. But don't despair—armed with a string trimmer, spade, and garden fork, you can transform it into a thriving vegetable plot over the next few months.

Potatoes
Planted before you moved in, these potatoes are a welcome find and can definitely stay to provide the first harvest of the year.

Path from reclaimed slabs
The existing slabs can remain in place for now since they make a sturdy path and will keep weed seedlings at bay.

Kitchen garden checklist

When you are first looking around a plot, consider the following:
◆ Is the rest of the yard neat and tidy? (You don't want weeds straying into your vegetables.)
◆ What is the access like?
◆ Is there a water supply nearby?
◆ Are there fruit trees, vegetable plants, and other items such as cold frames that can be salvaged?
◆ Is there room for a compost bin close by?

"Keep a lookout for anything that can be recycled."

Raspberries These canes are on the edge of the plot and can remain as a useful screen.

Area to renovate

Once the site has been cleared, choose an area to cultivate first. By starting in a small way, growing your own food will seem less daunting than if you try to cultivate the entire plot all at once. The owner of this garden (left) has decided to cultivate the area in the center first because it has nothing worth keeping and so can be cleared completely, while other areas of the plot have fruit trees and other plants. The previous owner has left some really useful material behind, including a railroad tie, which will make a great bench, and some old pieces of wood from which raised beds can be constructed.

Area to renovate The area in the center of the plot will make a good starting point, enabling it to be expanded later in the year. Once the area has been cleared of debris, it can be measured for some new raised beds.

Strawberry patch These can stay in place for now since they will suppress weeds and hopefully supply a good crop of berries in the summer. Next year, the younger plants can be lifted and planted in a new bed.

Raised beds Pieces of wood can be recycled to edge the vegetable beds.

Logs It may be possible to use these to create the legs for a bench.

Completely overgrown site

Your first task is to clear the weeds so you can see the bare bones of your site. Wear gloves and protective clothing since there could be broken glass, wasps' nests, bottles of chemicals, and other hazardous items lurking in the brambles. Start by either string trimming or applying a systemic weedkiller to eradicate the worst of the weeds. Watch for plants to save, and useful material such as wood. If it's too overwhelming, ask for help.

Keep anything useful Keep a lookout for anything that can be recycled, such as wood for raised beds or pallets for making compost bins.

Old raised beds may be salvageable.

Fruit bushes can be rejuvenated with pruning.

Different types of sites

Before planning your garden, first assess your site to determine which areas are sunny or shaded and for how long during the day, since this will affect the crops you can grow. Similarly, if your plot is at the bottom of a hill it may sit in a frost pocket, so you will need to grow hardier crops, or plant out only once the frost has passed. Plots at the top of hills can be cold and windy, which may rule out tall or tender crops.

SITE CHECKLIST

- Which direction does it face?
- Is it sunny for most of the day?
- Is it shady for most of the day?
- Is it exposed or sheltered?
- Does the ground slope?
- Are there potential frost pockets?
- Is there easy access to a water tap?

Orientation Use a compass to work out the direction your garden faces. South-facing sites are warm, north-facing are cool.

A clean slate Clearing an existing plot enables you to plan your crops to best suit the site and soil conditions.

If you have a sunny site

Sunny sites provide the best growing conditions, warming up quickly in spring and allowing the longest growing season. If you also have a wall or fence to provide shelter, fruit and fruiting vegetables, such as peppers, tomatoes, eggplants, cucumbers, and squashes, will do well, and root and salad crops will also flourish. The downside is that the soil will dry out quickly and you may need to water your crops more often, even twice daily during hot weather. Add well-rotted organic matter to the soil to help retain moisture, and mulch around crops regularly.

Exposure

The exposure, or direction your plot faces plays a vital role in how well your crops grow. It not only determines how sunny or shaded the plot is, and for how long during the day, but also affects the direction the wind blows from, and even how much rain it receives. While you can reduce the effects of exposures by removing shade-casting obstacles or by installing windbreaks, it is best to grow according to the conditions.

If you have a shady site

Shady sites are more limiting than sunny plots because most fruit and vegetables require some sun. They are also colder with a shorter growing season, which means sun-loving crops, such as tomatoes and eggplants, may struggle. Try to reduce the amount of shade by pruning overhanging trees, or move or remove obstacles that are casting shade. Opt for crops that don't mind some shade, such as potatoes, lettuce and salad greens, Jerusalem artichokes, and spinach. If you have sunnier areas on the plot, use these for crops that need brighter conditions.

If you have an exposed or hilly site

Plots on hills are often exposed and windy, although less prone to frost than those in valleys. To increase your choice of crops, and to improve their success rates, install a windbreak, such as a hedge, or an open-weave fence that allows some wind to pass through. Tall crops, such as sweet corn and fruit trees, may still suffer wind damage, so plant low growers instead, such as root crops, salad greens, and hardy fruit, like strawberries and raspberries. Wind also dries the soil very quickly, so make sure you install an efficient watering system.

If you have a site in a frost pocket

Frost pockets commonly occur at the base of hills, in valleys, and on north-facing slopes, or simply where the cold air can't escape due to walls, fences, or dense hedges. Frost can damage or kill plants, particularly young seedlings and emerging spring blossoms. It can also destroy crops in fall if they haven't been harvested soon enough. Protect plants by covering them with row cover and cloches. Delay planting outside until after the threat of frost has passed, and harden plants off fully. Keeping the net roofs on fruit cages can raise the temperature at night by a few degrees.

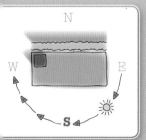

South-facing plot This is an ideal exposure for sun-loving crops, since the plot will not be shaded by neighboring trees, sheds, or hedges. The plot will be warm and bright.

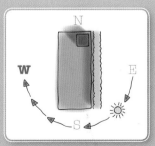

West-facing plot This garden will be bathed in sunshine for most of the day, except for early in the morning, when the sun will be rising from behind the hedge.

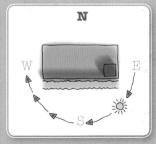

North-facing plot This plot could be shady if the hedge isn't kept low, since it will cast shade over the south side of the plot at midday. The shed will also cast shade.

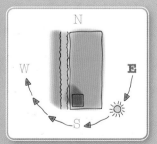

East-facing plot The west side of this plot will be in shade, so crops here won't benefit from the warm evening sun. The shed would be better sited at the north end.

step 2

preparing your soil

know your soil • what's in your soil • the acid test • improving your soil • clearing the weeds • fertilizers • double digging

sandy soil

clay soil

silty soil

alkaline soil

step 2 Know your soil

Is your soil dry and dusty, sticky and wet, or a crumbly mix of the two? Whatever your soil type, there are plenty of crops that will thrive on it, because some like free-draining sand, while others prefer nutrient-rich clay. There are also easy ways of improving soil to create the perfect loam that most crops love.

What's in your soil?

The type of soil you have in your garden is determined by the ground rock below it, and by the amount of organic matter, such as decayed plants, garden compost, and animal manure, that it contains. Most soils are either rich in sand or clay, while a few near coastal sites may be silty, and those over limestone rock are thin and alkaline. The best soils, known as loams, contain a mixture of clay and sand, and are easy to work, retain water and nutrients, and drain well. Although few of us are lucky enough to have loam, there are ways to improve all soils, whatever their composition.

◆ **TO DETERMINE YOUR** soil type, take a small sample in your hands and press it between your fingers. Clay soil will form a ball when rolled, while sandy soil feels gritty and falls apart when you try to roll it. Silty soil feels a little like clay, but has a more silky texture. If you have alkaline soil, you will see the white chalky deposits running through it and it will dry out quickly, like sand.

"Knowing your soil type will help you make the most of it."

Clay soil This is sticky and wet to the touch, and forms a ball when rolled between the hands.

Sandy soil This feels gritty and damp; it will simply fall apart if you try to roll it into a ball.

Silty soil This behaves more like clay, but it feels silky. It will also form a ball when rolled.

alkaline

acidic

THE ACID TEST As well as assessing your soil for its sand or clay content, you should also find out its pH value, which is a measure of its acidity or alkalinity. You can do this very easily with a pH kit. Simply add a small sample of soil to the liquid provided and the resulting color will show the acidic content of your soil. Most crops grow well in neutral to slightly alkaline soil, but you need acidic conditions to grow crops such as blueberries. If your soil is alkaline, simply grow acid-lovers in containers of acidic potting mix.

Acid-loving blueberries

Improving your soil

Successful fruit and vegetable growing is all about preparation. Before you sow a single seed, there is a lot of work to do. Once the soil has been cleared of weeds, it must be thoroughly dug over and leveled. If the soil is poor, it will need improving with organic matter before finally reducing the soil down to a fine tilth, or a nice crumbly consistency. Having done all this, you will be ready to sow your first seeds.

Remove large objects first

Before you put your garden fork into the soil, start by clearing the surface first, removing all garbage, broken glass, and large stones or bricks. Consider renting a mini excavator if there is a lot of large material to clear.

Clear the weeds

It is well worth spending time thoroughly clearing the site of weeds right from the start. Once seeds are sown and crops are planted, it becomes considerably harder to eradicate them from the plot. Use a fork to dig them out, since a spade can slice through perennial roots, encouraging them to multiply. Make sure you work the entire bed since weeds will spread very quickly if they aren't dealt with from the start.

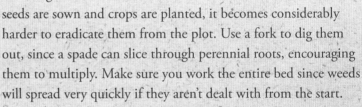

Pull out weeds Take care not to snap the roots when prying out perennial roots with a fork, or the weeds will quickly grow again.

Be thorough
Perennial weeds such as ground elder, couch grass, and dandelions will continue to grow if just a tiny piece of root is left in the ground. Dig deeply, because plants such as bindweed can have roots that extend as deep as 24in (60cm) into the soil.

Keep or discard
Take a careful look through the trash. Consider whether some of the material could be recycled. Wooden crates can make great containers for potatoes, while bricks or slabs could be used to make paths.

> "**Weeds** will spread if they aren't **eradicated at the start.**"

Dig over and level the site

Once the site has been cleared of weeds, use a spade to dig it over. Choose a spade that feels comfortable for you, is light, and of a suitable length. Avoid lifting too much soil on your spade each time you dig because it can damage your back. The soil should ideally be dug down to a depth of around 18in (45cm), ensuring that any compacted soil is broken up in the process.

Digging technique Keep your knees bent and your back as straight as possible to avoid injury.

Ready for improvement After removing weeds, the beds can be dug over using a spade. This loosens the soil and improves the consistency.

Double digging (see p.24) The bed should be dug over to twice the depth of the spade head. Fill the bottom 8in (20cm) with organic matter.

Leveling Once the soil has been dug over, it should be roughly leveled using a landscape rake or the back of a spade.

Fertilizers

It is probable that the soil of your plot will need improving if you are going to grow crops successfully. Adding organic matter to the soil after double digging will encourage the roots to penetrate deeply and find nutrients and water. However, young seedlings and shallow-rooting plants will need their nourishment to be closer to the surface. There is a wide range of materials that can be added to the soil and lightly dug into it afterward.

Barnyard material Add lots of organic matter to the surface. This helps to suppress weeds and improve the growing potential.

Compost Well-rotted garden compost will help to retain moisture around young seedlings and will be full of nutrients.

Chemical General-purpose fertilizers will provide young plants with a much-needed boost in the early stages of growth.

Project
Double digging

step **3**

Double digging is usually carried out if the ground has not been previously cultivated, or if drainage and soil structure need to be improved. It is worth the hard work and will result in better soil quality.

step **2**

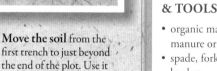

Move the soil from the first trench to just beyond the end of the plot. Use it to fill in the final trench.

MATERIALS & TOOLS

- organic matter: manure or compost
- spade, fork, rake, bucket

step **1**

1 Begin by digging a trench at one end of the bed to the depth of your spade and approximately twice as wide. Keep the width and depth consistent as you dig, and try to keep the sides as neat as possible. Remove any weeds and large stones you find.

2 Put the excavated soil from this trench into a large bucket or a wheelbarrow. This will be used to fill in the final trench at the end of the bed.

3 Dig and loosen the soil in the base of the first trench to another spade's depth, breaking up any big, hard lumps, and removing any stones or debris.

4 Now add well-rotted manure or compost to the bottom of the trench and lightly fork it in.

5 Dig the second trench directly adjacent to the first, and to the same dimensions. Use the soil dug out to fill in the first trench. Once again, remove any weeds, rocks, or other debris as you go.

6 Similarly, use soil from the third trench to fill the second, once organic matter has been forked in. Repeat this process all the way down the plot. Finally, use the soil set aside from the first trench to fill in the top layer of the last.

step 4

Why double dig?

For your garden plot to support healthy, vigorous crops, it needs to be well drained and aerated. Incorporating well-rotted organic matter will feed your crops and also improve soil structure. This technique is so named because each trench is dug twice; once to remove the top layer and any weeds, and a second time to loosen and aerate the sub-layer, and to introduce organic matter.

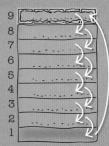

move trench 1 soil to the end

Dig the organic matter into the loosened soil at the base of the trench, so it is well distributed.

step 5

Keep the excavated trenches the same size, so the soil from one is enough to fill the previous one.

step 6

The soil deposited in the first trench will set higher than it was originally, but will eventually settle.

Dig over the base of the last trench in the same way as previous ones, and add manure or compost.

The soil saved from the first trench, here placed on the path, can now be used to fill in the final trench.

All that remains is to rake over the garden plot until a fine tilth is achieved. Avoid walking on the newly dug plot at first, or the soil will quickly become compacted.

step 3

creating your space

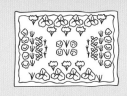

beds & borders • plan your space • choosing paths • materials for paths • marking out the area • prepare the edges • prepare the surface • raised beds

step 3

Beds & borders

Creating the beds and borders in your yard is an exciting stage in the development of your garden design. There are a number of practical considerations to take into account, but you can also allow the creative side of your brain to have a say and consider different shapes or use recycled, quirky materials to give it a personal touch.

Guide to bed size

The size of the beds is a matter of personal preference. However, it is important to be able to reach the middle of a bed without walking on the soil and compacting it, so it's sensible to restrict the width to about 3ft (1m). You can be more flexible about length, but remember you can fit in more crops if you have fewer paths.

- Beds should be narrow enough to reach into the middle.
- Paths should be wide enough to accommodate a wheelbarrow.

A good size These beds allow room for a range of crops, yet are narrow enough to work on without walking on the soil.

Position and types of beds

Deciding where the beds are going to be placed is key to the overall design of the plot. The most popular and simplest solution is to create beds directly in the soil. Access is important, so make sure you leave enough room between the beds to get your wheelbarrow up and down.

◆ **RAISED BEDS** are the perfect solution to gardening on poor soil. Once built and filled with good-quality soil mix, the benefits are enormous. There is no more backbreaking weeding, while planting and harvesting are made much easier. The extra height means the soil is well-drained and it warms up more quickly in the spring. Another benefit is that the crops will ripen more quickly.

Concrete slabs These large, heavy blocks make a very sturdy structure for edging the beds. Thanks to their weight, they may not need to be dug into the soil.

Log rolls Wood is a popular material for edging a bed. Make sure that the wood is suitable for outdoor use or it will rot quickly. Use stakes to secure it in place.

Edging stones For a more formal effect in the vegetable beds, use these attractive edging stones. Sometimes vintage stones can be acquired at estate sales.

"Get your plans and design down on paper."

Draw a plan Sketching out a plan of your plot is a very useful exercise that will help you to prioritize what you want to include.

Plan your space

Get your plans and design ideas down on paper. This is best done in the garden so that you can be accurate. You will probably make several drafts before you decide on what will work best for the space you have available. Don't worry about specific planting at this stage; this is just a rough sketch to determine the underlying structure of the plot. Think about where you want to create fruit and vegetable beds, where you want paths, a shed, a cold frame, compost bin, onion rack, and perhaps a seating or barbecue area, If you have a large yard, you may want to consider including a sandbox, children's toy area, or even a swing or slide.

Ideas for recycled raised beds

Almost any container or box can be used in the garden as a raised bed. Just ensure that the material is durable, weatherproof, and has adequate drainage to prevent plant roots from rotting.

Old sink Not only does this make a beautiful feature, but the plughole also makes the perfect drainage hole.

Drainage pipes These terra-cotta pipes are good and deep—ideal for growing vegetables with long roots.

Tires These are perfect for growing sweet peas. They can also work for potatoes—stack more on top as they grow.

Metal edging Beds edged in metal will give your garden an urban feel. Be aware, though, that they heat up in the sun, which can burn plant roots.

Wooden planks These are quick and easy to install and will do the job of keeping the soil mix in place, but they may not last as long as other types of edging.

Choosing your paths

Once the beds have been constructed, you can start to consider the layout and material for the paths. They need to be as functional as possible as this will enable you to work efficiently. Paths in your kitchen garden probably do not need to hold much weight and won't require cement or lots of hardcore as a base. This means they can usually be made using limited DIY or landscaping skills.

Materials to use

There is a wide variety of different materials that can be used to make paths, all of which can be quite costly to buy, so first take a look around to see what material can be recycled. Check local landscaping companies to see if they are throwing out old paving slabs, or see if you can obtain materials free via your local Freecycle website. Essentially, a path can be made of anything, including ornamental bark chip, bricks, or even carpet; the choice is yours.

♦ **GRASS PATHS** are probably the cheapest to make if you can't find anything to recycle. Not only do they provide a soft, durable and natural surface, but the seed is also very cheap.

Bricks These are one of the most durable materials for paths. They don't necessarily need cementing together, as long as they are bedded firmly into the soil.

Carpet scraps These make an attractive and surprisingly hard-wearing path, although they can be prone to rot after prolonged periods of cold, wet weather.

Bark chips Using a natural material such as this popular mulch gives a path a nice finish, but it needs to be edged to avoid the bark spilling onto the beds.

Artificial turf If you like the look of grass paths, but don't want to spend time mowing and edging them, then artificial turf could be the answer, but it is not a cheap option.

Use your plan to mark out the area Plan out where the paths are to go. They provide your route for moving around the plot, so they need to be practical, functional, and ideally take you straight from A to B.

Edging the paths

Hard landscaped paths should be finished with an edge to retain their structure and prevent loose material such as bark chips and gravel from spilling onto the beds. Grass paths don't require an edge, but will look much sharper if the sides are regularly clipped with edging shears and given definition each season with the edge of a spade.

String and bamboo stakes Use these to mark out where you want to create your paths. Take into account the areas where you are most frequently going to walk, which will include accessing rain barrels and compost heaps.

Bamboo stakes Insert these at the corners of paths and intersections; push them in far enough to take the strain of the string and ensure they are straight. Once they are in place, wind the string around them to give an outline of paths and beds.

Mark the perimeter Once the paths have been marked out, the soil should be leveled and all humps and bumps flattened out. The surface should be lightly trodden down and compacted to prevent the path from sinking at a later date.

Weed barrier Not the most attractive of materials, but it will suppress weeds and create a smooth surface. It looks better if covered with bark chips.

Gravel This material needs to be laid on a weed barrier and edged or it will eventually disappear into the soil. It is not easy to push a wheelbarrow on.

Deck boards Be careful not to slip on these boards since they can be treacherous when wet. Choose boards with grooves cut into them; alternatively, saw your own.

PROJECT Part 1
Paths: Mark out the area

To get the best use out of your garden, the paths and access routes should be well planned to make sure you can easily reach all areas of your plot.
The most heavily used routes will benefit from a properly constructed path which, as well as being practical, will improve the look of the whole area.

step 2

Make the frames

This garden (see right) has been set out with raised beds in the middle, with their frames also forming the edges to some of the paths. The bed frames and path edges are made in the same way using planks and stakes—assemble them on a workbench or any level area. Cut the wood sides to length and join them at the corners with screws, using simple butt joints (see below).Use only pressure-treated lumber, which resists decay, to prolong the life of your paths and beds.

Every corner joint and intersection should have a stake to support it.

step 1

Path stakes only need to protrude slightly higher than the edge, and can be trimmed later. Bed stakes that support nets should be longer.

Ensure bed corners are at right angles using a builder's square. Attach wood diagonals to support and hold the frames together.

Screw the joints Holding both sides of the bed frame or path edge steady, screw the joints together. You may find it easier to drill small pilot holes for the screws.

1   Mark out the plot using stakes and string as a guide, and temporarily place the bed frames in position. It's likely that they will not sit very squarely to begin with, so it may be necessary to level the soil surface using a rake or spade.

2   Once the beds and the path edges are in place, work out how many stakes are needed—one for each corner, and one every 5ft (1.5m) along the sides—and lay them out.

Pointed stakes

The stakes should be long enough to support the full height of the planks, plus a further 8in (20cm), which is driven into the soil. Before the stakes are hammered into the ground, it is useful to cut one end into a point to make the task easier.

Use a wooden or metal stake to form pilot holes. This will make it easier to drive in the stakes squarely. It will also help to pry buried stones out of the way.

Drive the stakes in as squarely as possible. Ideally, their tops should be level with the top of the wood they are supporting; they can be tapped in further or trimmed as required.

The top of the path edging should be a little higher than the soil level to prevent soil from falling onto the path.

3   Once you are satisfied with the layout of the paths and beds, begin to drive in the prepared stakes for the path edges.

4   Each stake should be driven into the ground to a depth of at least 8in (20cm), although this will need to be increased if the ground is soft and unsupportive.

5   With the beds still temporarily in place, line up the path edges against their stakes to finalize their positions. Some stakes may need slight adjustment so they line up properly.

MATERIALS & TOOLS

- lengths of treated lumber, wooden stakes, screws, string line, bamboo stakes
- hammer, straight metal bar, screwdriver, workbench, clamps, builder's square, spade, rake

...part two

PROJECT Part 2
Paths: Prepare the edges

Once the planning and initial preparation of the path edges is done, the area will begin to take shape. The stakes have been driven in, and the paths and beds have been planned. If your plot is on level ground, leveling and positioning of the edges is easy, but it will be more time consuming if the site slopes.

The existing path between this garden and the one next door was reasonably level, so it was used as the starting point. The first path edge was placed parallel to the existing path, and at a similar height.

Lay of the land

This particular site slopes gently and consistently from north to south. As a result, while some of the edges sit quite level, those at right angles to them will have to follow the existing ground level. As long as you bed the edges in well, the paths will be sturdy and practical.

To save lumber, you can join sections that are not long enough. An extra stake can be driven in at the joint, or use a scrap to overlap both ends and screw them together, as shown.

step 1

If there are paths that lead off the main path, remember to leave corresponding gaps in the edging. This will be easier than cutting them out later.

You may find that the wood available is usually no more than 15ft (5m) long. Since most gardens are longer or wider than this, some joints are inevitable.

1   First choose a level section of path edging and screw the wooden planks to the stakes. This can then be used as a starting point for the next section. Lay the edging against the stakes and adjust the height as necessary, comparing it to surrounding ground levels. Hold the wood edges in place temporarily with clamps, or prop them up with rocks. You may need to dig out areas where the soil level is too high.

step 2

2 With most of the path edges in place, the raised beds can be temporarily laid back into position to check their levels.

3 The side paths can now be fixed, using the main path as a guideline. Line up the edges to see if any soil needs to be removed before joining them together.

Attach path edges to the stakes where they meet at corners to create a strong joint.

With the frames back in place you can now see clearly how much, if any, soil needs to be removed to ensure that they sit neatly in position.

step 3

Ensuring that you do not push the frame out of line, drive the stake in flush to the edge of the board and screw together as normal.

step 4

You will rarely have spare soil in the garden; the excess soil from the paths is being used in the raised beds, or can also be used for many other purposes.

step 5

4 With the path edges in place, you may find you require additional stakes to hold them firm, especially if the site slopes.

5 Now that the paths are formed and the bed positions marked out, you can easily see where soil must be moved to level the paths and build up the beds.

 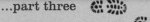

PROJECT Part 3
Paths: Prepare the surface

Now the path edges have been fixed into position, you are nearing the final stages of the project. This next step involves preparing the surface of the paths so they are durable and easy to maintain, and installing the frames for the raised beds. Once completed, the area will be transformed into a recognizable growing space.

step 2

Weed barrier tips

Once the weed barrier has been laid, a good way to prevent weeds growing along the sides of the paths is to tuck the barrier under the path edging. If the lumber sits tight on the soil, scrape some away, then tuck the sheeting underneath.

Use rocks or old bricks to hold the weed barrier in place while you continue to lay it.

step 1

Trim excess barrier once all the paths have been covered. Cut it using scissors or a utility knife.

1 Starting at a place where it is easy to work, lay strips of weed barrier along the paths, overlapping the sides where the raised beds will be sited.

2 Work your way over the whole area, covering the paths with barrier. You may need help to lay and hold the sheeting in position.

Tip bark chips or gravel onto the barrier once large sections of the path are covered.

step 3

To ensure the raised beds are level with the path edging, lay a piece of straight wood across them. Raise and lower the edges accordingly, then screw the framework to the stakes.

When secured, the raised bed frames will conveniently hold down the weed barrier. Any diagonal support braces on the frames can now be removed.

step 4

3 Place the raised bed frames in position, tuck the barrier beneath their sides, and screw them to their stakes.

4 With all the weed barrier tucked neatly under the path and bed edging, trim off any excess material. Cover the barrier with bark or gravel, leveling and compacting it in layers.

5 The path will eventually settle and may need topping off. Apply a fresh layer of bark or gravel each year, and remove any weeds that poke through.

Remove the rocks or bricks used to weigh down the barrier and rake out the bark or gravel to cover the paths. Try not to snag the surface.

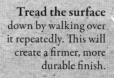

MATERIALS & TOOLS
- weed barrier or sheeting, bark chips or gravel
- utility knife or scissors, wheelbarrow, rake, shovel

step 5

Tread the surface down by walking over it repeatedly. This will create a firmer, more durable finish.

 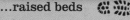

Project Part 4
Raised beds

The final stage of the project is to finish the raised beds and fill with soil, ready for sowing. The height you choose depends on what you want to grow, and how good the underlying soil is. Make deeper beds to grow root crops, or if the soil is poor. If the soil is decent quality or you are growing leaf and pea crops, create shallower beds.

The boards that comprise the frames for the raised bed should be screwed to each other, and also to the corner stakes.

step 1

step 2

step 3

1 The construction of the raised beds is the same as previously outlined (see p.32). However, depending on your growing requirements, their depth can be altered using wider or narrower edges. Scaffolding and decking planks are popular choices.

2 Once the frames are in place and have been securely fixed to the stakes, they can be filled with soil.

3 Rake the soil roughly level with the top of the boards, picking out larger rocks and any debris, and add well-rotted organic matter before planting.

MATERIALS & TOOLS

• wooden planks—recycled scaffolding planks or deck boards, lumber, screws, nails
• hammer, screwdriver, shovel, rake

Simple options

One of the benefits of raised beds is that you can make them to suit your needs, which also includes keeping them simple. Beds can be made of anything that will contain soil, and don't have to be permanent. Large rocks or old railroad ties can easily be placed on the ground to form temporary beds. Raised beds can also be bought as prefabricated kits and are simple to construct.

Temporary beds Large planters grouped together provide a simple way to make a short-term raised bed. Butt them up as close as possible.

Kits There are many types of raised bed kits to choose from, made of concrete (above), wood, woven panels, and plastic. Most just simply lock together.

This raised bed has long stakes at the corners, which enables the produce grown in it to be easily covered with netting.

A typical raised bed is around 6in (15cm) deep, but can be deeper. The supporting stakes have been cut level with the edging boards.

A ground-level bed has a useful wooden edge to provide a barrier between the soil and surrounding path, serving to contain the plants and soil within.

step 4

protecting crops

protection from wind, frost, & pests • rabbit-proof fencing • greenhouses & cold frames • make a cold frame • cloches

step 4

Protection from wind, frost, & pests

The delight of growing your own food can sometimes be diminished by the discovery that your crops have been destroyed. Pests such as birds and slugs are opportunists and will feast on your vegetables unless you get there first, while wind can reduce foliage to ribbons unless you have provided protection.

Cage the plot The simplest solution to protecting crops from birds is to net the whole plot.

Screening tips

Air circulation among your crops is healthy; it helps to prevent a buildup of pests and diseases, so it is better if a windbreak is permeable. Avoid screening with walls and fences but instead plant hedges or erect a trellis.

Trellis panels These will protect your plants from harsh winds while still allowing the air to circulate.

Low screening This will protect seedlings but the wind will pass over the top and may damage taller crops.

Windbreaks

Kitchen gardens are frequently close to the back door. This means that they are often afforded some protection from the wind. However, if they are on a hill or at the edge of the site, then crops can easily be damaged and even blown over. There are many ways to shelter your crops from strong winds and you may not even need to screen the whole plot, rather just the side that faces the prevailing wind.

Choose a windbreak that suits the height of your crops

Netting to protect against birds & insects

Keep a lookout for pests and try to predict their feeding habits. Sadly, they are often only noticed when it is too late and they have already inflicted irreparable damage. Birds are the worst offenders, attacking ripe fruit and emerging vegetable shoots and foliage. Cages offer the best protection and you can buy commercially produced cages to suit your individual needs. However, it is just as easy to make your own cages by lashing bamboo stakes together and draping the proper type of netting over the whole structure.

Squirrels Robust cages are needed to protect crops against squirrels because their sharp teeth and claws easily rip through netting.

Cabbage white butterflies Members of the cabbage family should be covered with fine-mesh netting to keep these pests at bay.

Birds Cover leafy crops with netting to prevent birds from ripping the lush foliage. This is the only certain way to protect vulnerable plants.

Rabbits (see Project, pp.44–47) Erect chicken wire around the plot and dig it down into the soil to keep rabbits out.

"Air circulation is healthy so windbreaks should be permeable."

Slugs & snails

These pests can strip seedlings of their foliage in a matter of hours. Surround plants with gravel, ceramic tiles, sand, or copper since slugs and snails don't like to crawl on these materials. Place beer-filled containers in the soil to attract them. Snails and slugs will fall in and can't escape.

Plastic collars

Copper barriers

Cabbage collar

Project Part 1
Rabbit-proof fencing

Rabbits graze a wide variety of plants and can cause a considerable amount of damage in vegetable and fruit gardens, usually overnight. If your plot is in an area known to have rabbits present, it is best to take preventive measures and install a rabbit-proof fence to protect your valuable produce.

step 3

Position the four corner posts first. Once these have been driven in, a string line can be pulled taut between them to act as a guide for the remaining posts. This will ensure that they are in line, which will make attaching the wire far easier, as well as looking neater.

step 2

Leave enough space for the garden gate to be fitted; it will need approximately ½in (1cm) extra on each side so that it can open and close freely.

The posts should go in to a depth of around 12in (30cm), but this is dependent upon how soft the ground is.

step 1

1 First ensure that the perimeter of the garden is free of obstacles, then make a pilot hole at each corner using a metal bar or thin stake, 12in (30cm) deep, and slightly less than the thickness of the fence posts.

2 Drive the corner posts into the pilot holes, checking to be sure they are level. Either use a sledgehammer, which may splinter the tops, or rent a post driver (see above), which won't, and will drive them in straighter.

3 Run a string line between the four corner posts as a guide, and position more posts along the length, spaced 6ft (1.8m) apart. Make a pilot hole for each one, as before.

step 4

Supporting posts

Corner posts and gate posts need to be especially rigid, because they will be taking the strain of the fencing wire when it is pulled taut, plus the weight of the gate. This can be achieved by using wider posts here, or by attaching diagonal braces (see p.196).

step 5

Digging the trench allows the fencing wire to be buried, preventing rabbits from digging under it.

Wearing thick gloves, roll out the wire up to and beyond the next corner post, keeping it as taut as possible. Fold out the lower 6in (15cm) to line the base of the trench.

4 Drive all the posts in firmly, so they move very little when pushed. Now dig a trench around the entire perimeter, 6in (15cm) wide and deep.

5 At the top of one corner post, nail or staple the chicken wire 3ft (1m) above ground level, with 12in (30cm) at the bottom to line the trench.

6 Using pliers, pull the chicken wire as taut as possible, or ask a friend to pull it the opposite direction to make it tight. Nail or staple the chicken wire onto the next corner post, repeating this on all sides.

step 6

MATERIALS & TOOLS

- round or half-round posts 5ft (1.5m) long, galvanized chicken wire 4½ft (1.3m) high—the maximum mesh size should be 1in (2½cm)—fencing nails, 4in (10cm) galvanized clout nails, treated boards for top rail, screws
- claw hammer, pliers, sledgehammer or post driver, metal bar or wooden stake, hand saw, screwdriver, bubble level

On the final post, cut the wire, fold the ends in, and nail it neatly onto the post to prevent snagging yourself on any sharp loose ends.

...part two

Project Part 2
Rabbit-proof fencing

With the fencing wire neatly nailed into position, the fence can now be made rabbit-proof. Installing a top rail prevents the wire from sagging between the posts, and also gives a neater finish. A close-fitting gate makes the plot easily accessible, but not to rabbits.

step 9

MATERIALS & TOOLS

- reclaimed gate, latch, gate hinges
- tools as on previous page

Compact the soil thoroughly at the base of the posts. Once complete, gently rake the surface to a level finish.

step 8

Clamp the top rail in place temporarily before securing with screws at least 2in (5cm) long. The joints between the top rails should meet at a post.

Scrape the excavated soil into the trench and rake it level. Ensure the wire fencing is well buried.

step 7

7   Use the previously excavated soil to fill in the trench and cover the bottom of the fence wire.

8   Once the trench has been filled and leveled, it will need to be compacted firmly. Tread the soil down with your heel, all the way around.

9   Mark the posts at around 3ft (1m) above ground level, using a string line as a guide, and line up the top rail. The fencing wire should come to about halfway up this rail, where it can be nailed in.

step 10

step 11

Cut the posts to the same height above the top rail to give the fence a neater finish, although this is not essential.

Fix the gate hinges in position. Use only one or two screws at first, to see whether the gate opens and closes properly, before driving in the rest of the screws.

10 Pull the chicken wire upward so it is taut, and nail or tack it to the inside of the top rail. Do this all the way around the fence before trimming the post tops.

11 Using scraps of wood as wedges, hold the gate in place, allowing as little space as possible at the bottom, while still being able to open and close it easily. The space on both sides should be equal. Mark the position of the hinges and drill pilot holes slightly smaller than the diameter of the screws being used.

Diagonal braces help to support the gate posts, and can also be used to strengthen the corners.

Rabbits are unable to scale the fence, and the wire buried below ground level will deter them from burrowing underneath. The fence also creates a neat appearance.

Greenhouses & cold frames

A greenhouse is a useful addition to any vegetable plot, allowing you to give crops a head start, grow tender varieties, and extend the growing season. Cold frames also allow crops to be started earlier and are ideal for hardening off seedlings before planting them in the ground outside.

Greenhouses

Greenhouses come in a range of sizes and materials, and can be adapted for growing a wide range of crops, even all year. New greenhouses can be expensive but it is possible to buy them locally secondhand, so check your local paper or online.

◆ **THE BENEFITS** of having a greenhouse are huge. They provide the perfect growing conditions to raise seedlings, enable you to grow a wide range of heat-loving crops, such as eggplants and chiles, and also double up as a potting shed, allowing you to work even if the weather is bad.

Summer shade This grapevine provides much-needed shade in the summer, preventing plants inside from being scorched or overheating. Shade netting or shade paint can also be used.

Provide perfect
growing conditions

Collect rainwater
from the roof

Plant directly into greenhouse borders

"a greenhouse allows you to grow heat-loving crops."

Cold frames

Some subdivisions do not allow greenhouses, limiting you to using cold frames or plastic mini-greenhouses, which, nonetheless, have many benefits. Cold frames are low to the ground and perfect for acclimatizing seedlings to outdoor temperatures after they have germinated. They can also be used to protect early sown crops in spring from frost, prolonging the growing season. Mini greenhouses tend to be tall and narrow, and just large enough to grow two or three indeterminate tomatoes, peppers, chiles, or eggplants.

Temporary covers Lightweight growing tents can be placed over crops outside, giving the benefits of a greenhouse on a small scale.

Mini greenhouse Where space is limited, collapsible plastic greenhouses are ideal for growing heat-loving crops, such as tomatoes.

Plastic covers The advantage of clear plastic is that, unlike glass, it doesn't shatter, making it safer when children are around.

Wooden frames

Cold frames can be bought as kits, but they are just as easy to make yourself. The base can be made from bricks or wood, and an old window frame can be used as the lid. These can be permanent or temporary features.

Kits Cold frame kits come in a wide range of sizes to suit your needs, and are usually quick and easy to put together.

Recycled Reclaimed window frames are ideal for making cold frames, as are glass cupboard doors and large picture frames.

Homemade (see p.50) This cold frame has been made from an old shed, and the lid was salvaged from an old greenhouse.

Project
Cold frame

A cold frame is an unheated box with a hinged glass lid that offers plants protection from rain, wind, and cold. They are most useful in spring for hardening off plants, but are also used for sowing seeds and winter protection. This one is made almost entirely of salvaged materials.

Ensure that the angled cuts match, otherwise the lid may not close properly. It is easier to mark the boards before removing them to cut.

step 3

Strengthen the top of the frame by screwing on four wood strips.

MATERIALS & TOOLS

- old window frame, scrap wood, 4 corner posts, handles, wood strips, screws, nails, hinges, weed barrier
- hammer, drill, screwdriver, staple gun, clamps, saw

step 2

The rear panel should be slightly higher than the front to make the most of the sun, and to ensure rainwater doesn't settle on the lid.

G-clamps are useful for holding the frame together squarely while the boards are screwed into place.

Slot the wood tightly together and screw into place. Brush any dirt off the slats.

step 1

1　The dimensions of the cold frame are dictated by the size of the lid, so measure it first. Saw the wood to length and cut the corner posts to the right height.

2　Assemble a pair of opposite sides first. This will make screwing together the final two sides far easier.

3　Having assembled the entire base of the frame, the top board on either side now needs to be cut at an angle so that the front is lower than the back.

step 4

Ventilation catch

It is vital that the cold frame can be easily ventilated, otherwise it will fill with stale air and overheat, causing plants to wither on hot days. The gap to allow for fresh air need not be more than about 2in (5cm).

Ventilation catch

An old hinge and a scrap of wood can be used to create a basic but effective ventilation catch.

step 5

The window frame can be slightly larger than the base to offer more protection at the edges from driving rain.

4   To keep weeds from growing up through the frame, staple a sheet of weed barrier to the base.

5   Attach the window to the frame with sturdy hinges. If the wood is not very thick, fit the hinges at the corners, screwing into the posts for maximum strength.

The hinged lid of a cold frame makes tending the plants very easy. The size and location of the frame needs to be carefully considered to ensure all areas can be easily reached.

Lid support

There are various ways of holding open the lid of the frame while tending the plants. A wood strip and a simple catch made from a block of wood have been used here, although a salvaged window catch would work just as well.

Window catch

Cloches

Cloches are traditionally used in the vegetable garden to protect seedlings that need a little extra warmth early in the season. They are also useful for warming the soil in spring before planting or sowing, resulting in faster growth compared to plants sown on uncovered soil.

Types of cloche

The word cloche means "bell" in French and although traditional cloches are bell-shaped, there are many shapes and sizes available. Most people use tunnel cloches, which consist of strong, clear plastic stretched over wire hoops. These can be made large enough to cover whole rows of crops.

◆ **VENTILATION** is important when using a cloche to prevent the plants from overheating when the sun comes out. Crops will also need extra watering, since the rain cannot reach the roots while the plants are growing under cover.

Bamboo cloches These open cloches are ideal for protecting plants from larger pests, such as birds and rabbits, and from wind damage.

Traditional glass cloches

Plastic tunnel cloche

Modern plastic dome cloche

Homemade cloches

Although cloches are widely sold and there are many designs to pick from, it can be just as easy to make your own, and is certainly more cost effective. Tunnel cloches are simple to make using lengths of old garden hose to form the structure, while small panes of glass can be propped together to provide an effective shelter for plants. Clear plastic bottles are ideal to cover small plants—just cut off the bases.

Storage system Keep your homemade bottle cloches tidy by threading them onto bamboo stakes stuck into the ground. This stops them from blowing around in the wind.

Homemade cloche made from old panes of glass and stakes

Bottle bases protect against pests

Project Hanging basket cloche

step 1

step 2

step 3

1 A simple cloche can be made from the frame of an old hanging basket. Wrap it in plastic or row cover and wire it to the frame.

2 Hold the polyethylene stretched reasonably tight and cut off the surplus material so that the cloche looks finished.

3 Place the cloche over seedlings for protection when frosty weather is predicted. Stake it down to hold it in place.

step 5

feeding & mulching

fertilizers & mulch • granular fertilizer • tomato fertilizer • making liquid comfrey • composting & compost bins • a recycled compost bin

Fertilizers & mulch

step 5

Keeping your plants well fed and mulched will encourage healthy plants, which in turn will provide you with abundant crops throughout the year. Adding fertilizers to the soil provides vital nutrients that may be lacking, particularly if other crops have been grown there previously. Mulching helps to improve the quality of the soil, suppresses weeds, and retains moisture.

Fertilizer Always wear gloves when spreading fertilizer on the soil and read the manufacturer's instructions. You may also need to wear a dust mask.

Mulching

A variety of materials can be used for mulching, including well-rotted manure and garden compost.

Mulch seedlings Use well-rotted manure or garden compost to mulch around young seedlings. This helps retain moisture and suppress weeds.

◆ **FRUIT TREES** and bushes are usually mulched in early spring. Take care that the mulch does not come into direct contact with the trunk, since this will eventually rot the tree, causing it to die. When applying mulch, spread it out in a circle to the edge of the leaf canopy and to a depth of 2in (5cm).

◆ **VEGETABLE BEDS** can be mulched in the fall when they are empty. This gives time for the mulch to rot into the soil before you plant again the following spring.

◆ **APPLY MULCH** around seedlings and other plants to retain moisture and prevent weeds from germinating.

Granular feeds

Add fertilizer to the planting hole of fruit bushes to ensure the plant has the necessary nutrients when it starts growing. Controlled-release fertilizer releases its nutrients as the soil warms up, while slow-release fertilizer is gradually released into the soil.

Sprinkle granular fertilizer into the hole

Position the plant in the hole

The feed will slowly dissolve into the soil

How to apply fertilizers

Fertilizers usually come in liquid, granular, or powder form. Liquid forms should be diluted in a watering can, while granules and powder are usually sprinkled from a measuring spoon at the recommended rate. Add fertilizer to the soil before you apply any mulch. Sprinkle it over the surface, then rake it in lightly before you sow seed. Always wear gloves when you are handling powdered and granular feeds, and always read the manufacturer's instructions carefully before use. Avoid feeding plants in direct sunlight because the combination of sun and fertilizer can scorch them.

Liquid Some powdered feeds need to be diluted in a watering can. Stir well with an old stick before applying the fertilizer.

Use a tube Some feeds can be poured down a tube or plastic bottle to ensure the liquid reaches the roots where the nutrients are needed most.

Raking in Before you do any planting, lightly rake a general-purpose granular fertilizer into the soil.

No nozzle Most fertilizers work best when applied to the roots. Use a watering can without a nozzle for precision.

> **"Tomato** fertilizer is high in potassium and can be used to **feed fruit** and vegetable plants."

Tomato fertilizer

This must be diluted with water in a watering can. It is high in potassium and can be used to feed all fruiting vegetable plants—not just tomatoes—in order to improve color and flavor. Start feeding plants weekly after the first flowers have appeared in summer.

Carefully measure out the feed

Add it to a clean watering can

Dilute to the recommended rate

Project
Liquid comfrey

Comfrey is regarded as something of a wonder plant. It can easily be made into a liquid fertilizer, packed full of essential nutrients to give to your vegetables. Plant a small clump and it will rapidly spread, providing you with an abundance of natural fertilizer for your plants.

MATERIALS & TOOLS

- comfrey plant, water
- two clean plastic milk jugs with lids, pruners, watering can, strainer

Ensure that the cuttings you take are no longer than the container you plan to use to store the liquid fertilizer.

step **2**

step **1**

Clean, plastic half-gallon (2-liter) milk jugs are ideal for this purpose. Insert five or six cuttings per bottle.

Easy to grow

Although comfrey can be grown from seed, it is far easier to grow it from cuttings. Fortunately, in a community of gardeners, you will easily and quickly find a source. Best of all are root cuttings, ideally planted while dormant. Even the weakest-looking cutting will grow with suitable care.

Comfrey is so easy to grow that it can be difficult to eradicate, should you choose to at a later stage. It is a very vigorous plant and, on smaller plots, it is best grown in large containers to keep it from spreading.

1 Leaves from an established comfrey plant can be harvested four or five times a year, late spring to fall. Cut stems that are about 8in (20cm) long to fit into a half-gallon (2-liter) milk jug. Stems can be harvested from anywhere on the plant because regrowth is usually fast.

2 Stuff the cuttings into the milk jugs, which should be clean, have tight-fitting lids, and necks large enough to squeeze the cuttings through. Jugs that have handles will make pouring easier later.

step 3

How to use

Comfrey fertilizer (often called comfrey tea) can be used much like any other liquid feed. Tomatoes and zucchini in particular benefit from its use, and the cut stems are traditionally used to line a trench before planting potatoes. It can also be used as an "activator" in your compost bin to speed up the breakdown of the contents.

step 4

Store for four to five weeks; the leaves will rot down and the mixture will be very pungent.

3 Fill the bottle with tapwater to within an inch of the top.

4 Close the lid tightly and give the bottle a good shake, making sure all the leaves have been agitated.

5 After a month or so, strain the liquid to remove the foliage and pour the liquid into clean, plastic containers to store for use in the garden plot.

step 5

You may find it easier to strain the comfrey feed into a watering can and then to pour it into clean containers.

Before using, dilute the comfrey feed to about 1 part fertilizer, 10 parts water. The darker the feed, the more you should dilute it.

step 5 Composting & compost bins

Well-rotted compost is an essential ingredient for the garden. Whether dug in or used as mulch, it lightens up clay soils, improves moisture retention on sandy soils, and supplies valuable nutrients to your crops. It takes time to get a composting system going and it may be months before your first batch is ready, so start as soon as you can.

Why compost?

There are many good reasons to make your own compost, the most obvious being that it provides an excellent soil

Useful screening Compost bins can look unsightly, but are easily screened with a trellis, flowers, or by climbing crops, such as beans.

improver, better than any you can buy, and is almost completely free. Composting also provides the means to easily dispose of kitchen waste, lawn and hedge clippings, and plant debris from the garden that you would otherwise have to throw away. Making your own compost means you know what is going into the soil, and ultimately into your plants, which is important if you eat your crops. Compost heaps also provide a habitat and will attract beneficial insects, such as beetles and centipedes.

Correct proportions
When making compost, aim to mix two parts carbon-rich materials, such as dried leaves and wood chips, with one part nitrogen-rich leafy material, such as grass clippings and plant waste.

Turning the heap

Compost heaps should be turned about once a month to incorporate air into the material, which speeds up the process of decomposition. Turning involves digging out the material at the bottom of the heap and placing it on top. The compost is ready to use when it is dark brown, with a crumbly soil-like texture, and has a smell like damp woodland. It should not smell unpleasant or feel slimy.

Turning the compost

DO'S & DON'TS

- Do have more than one compost bin ready to use.
- Make sure compost is covered to prevent material from washing away.
- Turn the compost once a month.
- Add water to the heap if it appears dry during the summer.
- Don't add diseased plant material.
- Don't add meat or cooked food.

Types of bins

There is a wide range of compost bins available to buy, usually made of plastic or wood. They either come as kits or ready-made. Choose a size and design that suits your needs—have two bins if possible, so you can be emptying one while filling the other. Some communities provide compost bins free or at a discounted price, so make inquiries before buying your own. Compost bins are also easy to make. All you need is a large, sturdy container that will hold the material but also will keep out excess rainfall, allow air to circulate, and provide drainage at the base.

Recycled This compost bin was built from old wooden pallets. It is easy to make, taking about an hour. (see Project, pp.62–63)

Sectional Some compost bins consist of interlocking sections that can be stacked up gradually as more material is added to the heap.

Drum types These large, plastic bins are a popular choice. They are easy to set up and come with a lid and an access hatch at the base.

Tumble bins This type of bin is designed to rotate. The tumbling action mixes the contents with air and accelerates the composting process.

Slotted bins The holes in this plastic compost bin allow the air to circulate, which speeds up the process of decomposition.

Recycled tires If you can obtain free tires, it is cheap and very simple to make this bin by stacking them in a pile.

Mini tumbler This small, rotating bin is ideal for making compost quickly where space is limited. Turn the drum once a week.

Construction bags Green waste will rot down in most containers. These strong, woven, plastic bags are useful for creating good compost.

Project
Compost bin

Making your own compost is the best way of recycling garden and kitchen waste, and no garden is complete without at least one compost bin. Well-rotted compost makes an excellent soil improver, and will keep your plot fertile and productive. This compost bin is made with recycled materials, and is very easy to construct.

Fix wooden supports at the corners of the bin to prevent the sides from pushing apart. Use a G-clamp to hold them in place, then screw them in firmly

step 3

MATERIALS & TOOLS

- four pallets, ideally the same size, two gate hinges, scraps of wood or planks, selection of screws
- screwdriver, hammer, G-clamps, hand saw

step 2

Have a friend hold the pallets in place, although if the ground is reasonably level, they should stand up on their own.

Most pallets have chunky blocks at each corner. These are ideal for driving screws into, offering more support than the thin planks.

step 1

1 Find a suitable and accessible location for the bin, then roughly level the ground to make sure that the pallets will stand level, and position the four pallets in place.

2 Once you are satisfied that the pallets are setting squarely, drive two or three heavy-gauge screws in at each corner, top and bottom, making sure that the pallets line up neatly at the edges.

3 Strengthen the joints using wood scraps, screwing them in place. When the bin is full, there may be considerable weight inside the compost bin, so it should be properly supported.

step 4

Carpet cover

To prevent the contents of the compost bin from getting too wet, cover the top using a tarp or, for this project, some old carpet. Simply drape it over the top and secure it in place with some string so it does not blow away. In warm spells, remove the cover and check that the compost hasn't become dry, and add water if necessary.

step 5

Ensure that the access hatch opens and closes easily. To hold it shut, drive a stake into the ground in front of it (see above) or place bricks or large stones there.

4 This particular bin has a hinged door at the bottom of one side to give easy access to the compost when it is ready.

5 Cut off the lower portion of one pallet to serve as the hatch, and use a sturdy pair of gate hinges to reattach it.

6 Finally, attach a rudimentary catch to hold the hatch open when the compost is removed. A piece of wood held in place with a single, loosely tightened screw is ideal.

step 6

The door, once fully opened, can be held in place with the wooden catch, which simply swivels into place.

Although pallets are very sturdy, they will gradually decay, especially when used to make a compost heap. Check the joints every year, and if the structure seems to have weakened, build a replacement. Avoid using treated wood, which may taint the compost.

watering & weeding

watering **methods** •
water supply • weeds
& weeding • **disposing**
of weeds

Watering methods

Fruit and vegetable plants depend on regular watering in order to grow. Lack of water is the most common reason for plants dying. During dry periods in the summer it may be necessary to visit the garden twice daily to check on young seedlings and water them. Install water-saving devices such as rain barrels to maximize water conservation.

Rain barrels Collect rainwater by attaching gutters to the shed or greenhouse roof, and attach downpipes that feed into rain barrels.

Water tank and cistern Some garden sites have a water tank with a cistern. Every time water is scooped out, it automatically refills itself.

Getting it right

Giving your plants the right amount of water is critical. They will die if they don't receive enough, yet they can also suffer if they are overwatered. If fruit is overwatered it can split, particularly when close to harvest time. Vegetables often rot in damp conditions, and seedlings can suffer from fungal diseases. The simplest way to see if your plant needs watering is to stick your finger in the soil; if it feels dry, then it needs water. Give plants a thorough soak every few days to ensure that water gets right down to the deep roots.

Water spigot Many gardens are planned with a spigot nearby, where hoses and irrigation systems can be connected, making watering easier.

Better watering

On hot days, water in the morning or the evening when it is cooler. This gives the moisture an opportunity to soak slowly into the soil. Watering at midday in full sun can cause the leaves to scorch, and water quickly evaporates rather than soaking in. Check the individual requirements of your crops because some don't like alkaline water. This is particularly the case with blueberries and cranberries, which should only be watered with rainwater. The soil type, especially its ability to drain, also affects how often plants will need to be watered.

Watering with a nozzle Watering cans are useful for controlling how much water is given to individual plants. Attach a fine nozzle to the spout to give a gentle flow, ideal when watering young plants.

Puddle watering Creating a hollow bowl around plants acts as a reservoir, allowing water to pool at their bases and slowly soak down to the roots. However, make sure that the roots are still covered by soil, otherwise they will dry out even more quickly, and can be eaten by pests.

Using a hose This is the quickest method of watering large areas, but it can be wasteful. Direct the hose at the base of each plant so the water reaches the roots and doesn't splash wastefully off the leaves.

Using a homemade funnel Cut the bases off plastic bottles and bury the mouth-ends in the soil, next to plants. This creates a funnel that will channel the water directly to the roots.

Additional help

There are various irrigation methods and devices available to make watering easier. They help if you can't water the garden every day.

Bottle reservoirs Make holes in the caps of water-filled bottles and leave them to drip into the soil.

Pouch reservoirs This method involves a large water-filled pouch suspended over crops that slowly waters them via a thin tube.

WATER WISELY

- Check whether the soil is dry to avoid water wastage.
- Water in the morning or evening.
- Install rain barrels to minimize using tapwater.
- Don't waste water—only water around the root system of your plants.

step 6 Weeds & weeding

Weeds are a bane of the garden grower's life, competing with crops for water, nutrients, and light. Keep them under control, because they can smother smaller crops, and can be hard to eradicate once established.

Preventing weeds

It is impossible to avoid weeds in the garden, particularly if they aren't being controlled in neighboring yards from where they can easily spread. To help prevent them, cover any bare areas of soil, such as paths, with weed barrier. On new beds, consider covering the soil with black plastic and plant your crops through it. Regular mulching deters weeds and also feeds your crops so they are less affected by the competition. Cultivating the soil also helps to limit weeds. Although this brings weed seeds to the surface, where they will germinate, the seedlings will soon be unearthed and dug into the soil. Routine weeding also helps prevent future weeds by keeping them from setting seed.

PERENNIAL WEEDS

Perennial weeds regrow each year from their root system and are the hardest to get rid of. Most have a deep root system and include:

- dandelion
- bindweed
- thistle
- perennial nettle
- ragweed
- dock

ANNUAL WEEDS

Annual weeds grow, set seed, and die within a year. They usually have a shallow root system and are easy to hoe off or dig out. They include:

- hairy bittercress
- shepherd's purse
- groundsel
- annual meadow grass
- goosegrass

Hoe This is used for removing shallow-rooted weeds. Pull it through the surface of the soil toward yourself.

Hand fork This small tool can be used for digging out weeds without damaging the roots of adjacent vegetables.

Dutch hoe Push this hoe through the surface of the soil to sever the stems of shallow-rooted weeds.

Composting

Annual weeds can be put in the compost heap immediately, although avoid adding any that have set seed. Perennial weeds can be composted, but must be completely dead first.

Leave weeds to dry After hoeing, annual weeds can be left in the sun for a few days to dry out before disposing of them.

Collect the weeds Avoid immediately adding freshly dug up perennial roots to the compost, since they will regenerate and spread in the heap.

Speedy removal Hoeing is a quick way to remove annual weeds. Use a long-handled hoe to reach into the beds easily.

Dry in the sun (see Project, p.162) Perennial weeds should be collected and left on a rack to dry in the sun for a few weeks before being added to the heap.

"weeds are a bane of the garden grower's life, competing with crops."

Dandelion grubber Dandelions have a deep taproot, which should be removed entirely to prevent it from resprouting.

Garden fork Use a fork to dig out perennial weeds. A spade may slice up the roots, making the problem worse.

Hand weeding Weed between individual plants by pulling the weed seedlings out by hand. Pull them before they establish.

step 7

what to grow

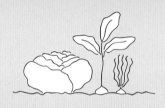

crops to suit your soil
& exposure • soil quality
• choosing crops •
flowers for cutting

step 7

Which crops will suit your soil & exposure

Some plants have specific requirements and will only grow successfully if they have the right conditions. Take time to check what they need and carefully read labels on seed packets and plants to ensure you are planting them in an environment where they will thrive.

Luxuriant leaves To produce a healthy crop like this, carefully check the soil and light levels in your garden before planting.

Soil quality

Do not worry if the quality of your soil is not ideal; it can be improved by adding organic matter, such as well-rotted manure or garden compost. Poorly draining soil can be improved by adding horticultural grit and sand. If excess alkalinity is the problem, there is very little that can be done to make the soil suitable for acid-loving plants, such as blueberries. The best solution is to grow acid-lovers in raised beds or containers, where you can then provide them with the perfect soil. Raised beds can be made cheaply from recycled material and are easy to construct, while a bonus with containers is that they can be moved in and out of the sun as required.

Alkaline soil

Where the soil is acidic, some plants are unable to access certain nutrients in it, which will lead to poor plant growth. Lime can be added, which will make the soil more alkaline, and increase its pH. If you are unsure what the pH of your soil is, buy a simple test kit.

The cabbage family, including broccoli and Brussels sprouts, likes an alkaline soil, making it less prone to clubroot (see p.235).

Acidic soil

Some plants will only grow in acidic soil. If your soil is very alkaline, the plants will need to be grown in containers or raised beds filled with acidic potting mix. If the soil has a neutral pH or lower, then it may be possible to acidify it with sulfur chips.

Blueberries are very particular and will only grow in acidic soil with a pH lower than 5.5.

Cranberries have similar acidic requirements to blueberries, but prefer very damp soil.

Potatoes are less prone to the fungal disease, potato scab, when grown in slightly acidic soil.

Full sun

Most plants prefer full sun. Mediterranean-type plants, such as tomatoes, peppers, eggplant, and squashes in particular need lots of light and warmth. Don't forget that plants in the sun also require plenty of water.

Eggplant must be harvested while the skins are still shiny.

Tomatoes are easy to grow and will bear fruit all through summer.

Peppers will grow well in pots if space is at a premium.

Chiles add color to the kitchen garden and are easy to grow.

Strawberries will fruit from late spring until the first frost.

Basil is an annual herb that you can easily grow from seed.

Apples are available in hundreds of varieties, some on dwarfing rootstock.

Pears taste most flavorful if eaten within days of picking.

Peaches should be fan-trained on south-facing walls.

Figs fruit more freely if the roots of the tree are restricted.

Shade

A few plants will tolerate light shade or even full shade. Gooseberries, cooking apples, and red currants will grow well on north-facing walls, while rhubarb is ideal for a shady corner of the garden. Leafy crops and the cabbage family will cope with moderate shade.

Gooseberries are sweetest when harvested in early summer.

Red currants can be planted against a wall if space is limited.

Cooking apples can be grown in shadier sites than dessert apples.

"Leafy crops cope well with moderate shade."

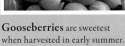

The cabbage family will provide a crop all year round.

Swiss chard can be harvested as a baby leaf crop or as mature leaves.

Choosing crops

The most exciting aspect of having your own garden is choosing what delicious fruit and vegetables you are going to be growing for your family and friends. Seed companies and garden centers have a huge range of crops available to suit everyone's personal taste. Be adventurous and grow things you would never find in a supermarket.

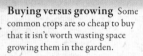

TO GROW...	easy
TO BUY...	expensive
SPACE NEEDED...	small

Buying versus growing Some common crops are so cheap to buy that it isn't worth wasting space growing them in the garden.

You can save yourself a fortune by growing some of the crops that are expensive to buy, yet can be grown easily for the cost of a few packets of seeds or plants. Year after year and for very little outlay, you could be picking an abundance of those delicious crops that you consider a real luxury. For example, raspberries are very expensive to buy, yet you will be able to harvest plenty if you grow your own. Similarly, zucchini produce huge crops from just one plant but are costly in the supermarket.

beets

lettuce

raspberries *snow peas*

- beets
- fava beans
- Brussels sprouts
- broccoli
- celery root
- zucchini
- green beans
- herbs
- leeks
- lettuce
- snow peas
- peas
- mixed salad greens
- purple and white
  sprouting broccoli
- radishes
- string beans
- green onions
- shallots
- spinach
- spinach beet and chard
- turnips
- soft fruit
- rhubarb

green onions

"cheap to grow, expensive to buy"

	TO GROW...	easy
	TO BUY...	cheap
	SPACE NEEDED...	large

Some crops found in abundance in the store are often extremely cheap, and therefore may not be worth the effort of growing yourself. Storage potatoes, for example, take up a lot of space and, although there are some great varieties available, you may decide that your space could be better used by planting more unusual or expensive-to-buy crops. Onions are another example of a crop that is inexpensive in the grocery store and takes up a lot of space. Consider your priorities carefully before deciding which crops to grow.

cabbage
garlic
onions
parsnips
sweet potato

- cabbage
- carrots
- celery
- garlic
- onions
- melons
- outdoor tomatoes
- parsnips
- peas
- potatoes
- pumpkins
- squash
- cauliflower
- rutabagas
- sweet potatoes

"**cheap** to buy so less worth growing"

	TO GROW...	varied
	TO BUY...	you can't
	SPACE NEEDED...	varied

There are certain specialty crops that you just won't find in the store. This is usually because they have a limited shelf life or because farmers don't consider it worthwhile growing them, but many are worth trying. Japanese wineberries, for example, produce tiny, delicious, blackberrylike berries that have the sweetest flavor ever. Zucchini blossoms don't last long enough to sell in the stores, but can be picked and fried in batter.

Romanesco broccoli

- beet leaves — earthy spinach substitute
- Chinese artichokes — hard to harvest commercially, but easily grown at home
- zucchini blossoms — too fragile to be transported
- hop shoots — used like asparagus
- Japanese wineberry — small fruit, costly to pick
- Asian flowering kale — flowers deteriorate quickly after picking
- pea tendrils — costly to harvest and pack
- radish seedpods — good for snacks and stir-fries
- Romanesco broccoli — easily bruised in transit
- sorrel — costly to pick
- tomatillo — doesn't get blight
- unripe wheat berries — used in some recipes

zucchini blossoms

"**money can't** buy these."

Flowers

Growing a range of flowers alongside your fruit and vegetable crops in the garden has many advantages. Not only will the flowers attract many beneficial pollinators that will also visit your other crops, but you will also have a supply of cut flowers for the house. You can grow your flowers in dedicated flower beds or among your fruit and vegetables, where they will add color, beauty, and scent to your plot.

Sweet peas and lavender
Sweet peas growing up stakes and lavender used as underplanting will waft their scent up in the air.

Companion planting Flowers can be grown as companions to vegetable plants, making the vegetables healthier by deterring pests and diseases from attacking the crops. Companion flowers will also attract pollinating insects.

Shrubs and climbers

Shrubs and climbers can be used to add height and permanent structure to your garden. Roses are perfect, with rambler types scrambling up trellises and through flower beds, giving the garden a wild and rustic feel, while shrub roses and hybrid tea roses can be used as cut flowers or left to simply beautify the area. Winter-flowering shrubs are especially welcome because they attract pollinating insects to the site.

◆ **PERENNIAL PLANTS** are a good investment since, once-planted, they will appear each year before dying back during the winter and reappearing in spring. They can be grown as cut flowers or to scent the area and make it look pretty.

◆ **ANNUALS** are perfect for creating a quick splash of color for the cost of just a few packets of seeds. There is a very wide range of plants to choose from, including favorites such as sweet peas and sunflowers, both of which are great for cutting.

Flowers for cutting

If you are growing flowers to cut for the house, it is easier to grow them in a "cut flower" bed rather than mixing them with other plants. Most flowers require fertile, rich soil if they are to bloom prolifically, so add plenty of organic matter. Choose a range of varieties, and you can have cut flowers for most of the year.

◆ **SPRING FLOWERS** could include daffodils and tulips; good summer choices are cosmos, roses, gladioli, sunflowers, and sweet peas; flowers for fall are asters, mums, and dahlias; and for winter, holly for berries and witch hazel for stems.

Personalize your plot with flowers

Flowers are an expression of your personality, and with such a range of shrubs and perennials, it's easy to find an assortment that you will love. Plant them around seating areas to enjoy them in your down time.

Flowers for cutting If you are growing flowers for cutting, it is easier to reach them if they are grown in rows. Remember to label them with their name and the date they were sown.

POLLINATION

Most flowers attract pollinating insects, but some do the job better than others.

- **AVOID** double flowers since bees cannot get inside the flowers easily.
- **SELECT** a range of flowers that will provide blooms for most of the year.
- **CHOOSE** native flowers and avoid bedding plants.
- **PICK** flowers that are blue, purple, violet, white, and yellow—bees have good color vision and are particularly attracted to these.

Hide your compost bin

As well as adding scent and color to your garden, flowering shrubs and herbaceous perennials can be used to screen unsightly areas such as compost bins, cold frames, and polytunnels. Ideally, choose evergreen plants like sarcococca and holly, because these will create a year-round screen. Alternatively, erect fences or trellis made from recycled materials and grow climbers such as honeysuckle, roses, and clematis up them. For summer screening from eyesores, grow tall flowers, such as rows of delphiniums, verbascums, sunflowers, or sweet peas.

step 8

creating a style

your style • seating & socializing • making a bench • herbs & the kitchen garden • children • an herb parterre • chickens & bees

Your style

One of the exciting aspects of having a garden is the chance to stamp your individuality on it. Your style can be as unusual and different as you like, the only restriction being your imagination. Revel in the freedom of creating something that's you, then sit back and enjoy the results.

Polytunnels Used to grow crops that need extra protection, a polytunnel also adds a laid-back feel to the garden.

Define your style

Choose a style that will suit your personality. Instead of following design advice in books word for word, look within yourself for inspiration. Are you a formal or informal sort of person? Do your tastes veer toward the modern or the traditional? Some people like to have everything perfectly manicured, with vegetables standing in immaculate straight lines and pristine bamboo stakes geometrically spaced one to the next. Others like a riot of color and shape, with beds overflowing with an abundance of vegetables, flowers, and fruit. Yet others like to reflect their nationality or culture, perhaps growing crops that are traditionally eaten in their country of origin, or personalizing their plot with anything from a garden gnome to a seated Bhudda statue.

Geometry and texture The strong geometrical shape of this parterre creates a modern and contemporary feel, while the textural foliage of the herbs and edible crops adds a sensory dimension to the design.

Formal or informal? These cabbage heads in perfect straight lines add a touch of formality to the plot, but the purple and green also add a creative contrast of colors.

Mixing styles The style of this kitchen garden is informal with plenty of plants packed closely together, yet the stark, sharp lines of the patio create an interesting contrast.

Community

If you're not sure you have time to manage your own garden, or don't feel confident about your horticultural skills, then you could consider getting involved with a local community garden. These are shared spaces where you garden on a communal piece of land in your area with other like-minded individuals. It's a fantastic way to meet new friends, pick up tips, and, of course, take home your own fruit and vegetables, without the responsibility of maintaining an entire garden.

Style compromise Working in a community garden means tailoring your style ideas to suit everyone else involved.

Seating & socializing

Growing your own is not all about hard work, digging, and weeding; socializing and having fun with family, friends, and fellow gardeners helps to maintain a balance between work and play, and is one of the major perks of having a garden. Create comfortable seating areas for you to take well-earned breaks and entertain others.

Making new friends

Organize an event in your garden with other gardening aficionados to get to know your like-minded neighbors. Meeting with others is a great way to exchange seeds and plants, but is also a valuable opportunity to get tips from some of the more experienced growers. Make sure you always have an extra cup of coffee in the kitchen for impromptu chats with other folks working outdoors.

Time out Take time to relax in the neighborhood and make new friends. Invite neighbors over for a barbecue or even ask them to give you a hand with a job in return for your helping them out with one of theirs.

PROJECT Bench

Make sure that the tops of the logs are level with each other so that the plank seat will set flat without rocking.

Use lengths of lumber to hold the logs in position temporarily, keeping the logs level and upright; remove once the concrete has cured.

step **1**

step **2**

step **3**

1 It is important to do a trial run to see where your garden seat fits best. You should also ensure the logs are long enough to allow about 12in (30cm) to be bedded in concrete below ground.

2 Allow an additional 2–3in (5–7.5cm) around the outside of the logs for the concrete bed, and a similar depth beneath.

3 Firmly pack the concrete around the circumference of the logs,

working to minimize air pockets, then smooth the top with a trowel 2in (5cm) below ground level to leave some space for bark chips or similar material to cover the concrete when dry.

Storage and seating This recycled old toolbox combines a handy storage space with a useful seating area that allows you to take a break from working in the garden.

Placing your seats

Think carefully about where you want to place your seating areas. If your dream is to have a quiet, secluded place where you can spend your weekend afternoons resting in the midday sun, you will need to make a space somewhere in a quiet corner out of sight of the prying eyes of passersby. However, if you like perching on a bench, watching the world go by and chatting with neighbors as they go about their business, then a prominent seat near the sidewalk will be a better choice for you.

Sunny spot Before creating a seating area, check to see whether it is in the sun or shade. Consider building screens and overhead pergolas if you are not a sun lover.

Time to relax Consider old-fashioned deck chairs for your seating. They are comfortable to lie back in and you can easily fold them up and store them in the shed.

Positioning Lay your seat across the logs and mark it with the locations of the two heavy-duty screws that must be drilled into each log. Drill a pilot hole for each one and tighten the screws fully with a wrench so that the heads are just a fraction below the surface of the seat.

Cozy corner Everybody needs the occasional slice of peace and solitude, away from the madding crowd. In this garden, the owner has erected recycled fence panels to create a private seating area.

Herbs & the kitchen garden

Growing herbs adds another dimension to the garden. When used in formal parterres, they can create rich tapestries of colors and patterns. They can also be grown for their beautiful flowers, for culinary use, or simply for their aromatic qualities.

Where to grow herbs

Herbs can either be grown separately in an herb garden or interplanted among vegetables and flowers. Fennel, with its stately umbels, blends in beautifully in a flower bed. Low-growing plants such as chamomile and thyme make attractive underplanting around the base of fruit trees, or they can be used to create herb lawns and paths. Many herbs have useful medicinal properties, but make sure you seek professional advice before using them to cure ailments. In terms of design, the huge range of textures, colors, and shapes exhibited by herbs provides an exciting palette for gardeners to use.

Edging Herbs such as rosemary, lavender or, in this case, chives, can be used to edge beds or weave intricate patterns to form strong structures and geometrical shapes.

"**In** formal parterres **herbs** create rich **tapestries** of **colors** and **patterns.**"

A lettuce parterre The interplanting of herbs and lettuce creates a garden that is pleasing to the eye as well as good to eat. Keep sowing lettuce in pots so you can replace those you have harvested.

Edging with boxwood (see Project p.87) Boxwood is the most commonly used plant for edging parterres and herb gardens since it is compact and evergreen. Prune when the risk of frost is over.

Children

Gardening is a wonderful hobby to do with your children. Not only does it provide some great physical exercise, but it also teaches them about where food comes from and inspires them to eat a more healthy and varied diet.

Containers Start children off with small growing spaces, such as containers filled with potting mix; that way they will not get overwhelmed by a large space.

Garden with friends Children love the social aspect of learning how to garden. There's nothing more fun than getting messy in the dirt with friends.

How to inspire children

Children like to see quick results so choose fast-growing crops such as "cut-and-come-again" salad greens, radishes, and green onions. Also, get them involved with choosing food they will enjoy eating, such as strawberries, raspberries, carrots, and potatoes.

◆ **MOST CHILDREN LOVE** the messy aspects of working in the soil, so consider setting up a worm compost or getting them to turn the soil. They also enjoy picking all the slimy slugs, snails, and even caterpillars off the plants. Many schools have after-school clubs, which is a fantastic way to get children excited and inspired about growing their own food. Volunteering with them is also a great opportunity to pass on your newly acquired culinary and horticultural expertise to the next generation.

Safety first

Make sure the garden is a safe place for children to work and play. Check the site and remove any broken glass or tripping hazards. Cover the ends of bamboo stakes to prevent eye injuries. Here are some creative methods of adding protection (see right).

Plastic connector

Flexible tubing

Small bottles

Snail shells

Project
Herb parterre

A traditional parterre is an ornamental herb, flower, or vegetable bed edged with low, tightly clipped evergreen hedging. This is a novel way to introduce some variety and additional color to your garden, while remaining practical and providing a good opportunity to grow some useful culinary herbs.

This parterre follows a very simple yet practical design, providing four triangular beds for the herbs.

step 1

step 2

step 3

1   Prepare the bed thoroughly by digging in plenty of organic matter, then cover the plot with a generous layer of well-rotted compost and rake it over so it looks fine and crumbly.

2   Having decided on the plan of your parterre, partition off the plot using bamboo stakes and run string lines across to section it off.

3   Do a trial run before planting, placing plants on the ground and moving them around until you are happy with the final layout.

Planting mint

Mint is often found in herb gardens, and its leaves add flavor to many recipes. However, be careful where you plant it because it is very invasive and can take over the whole garden. To contain its fast-growing and vigorous roots, plant mint in a submerged pot, leaving the top of the pot slightly above ground level.

step **4**

step **5**

MATERIALS & TOOLS
- string line, bamboo stakes, bucket, selection of plants
- hand trowel, tape measure

Careful planning should ensure that once the herbs reach maturity, a fairly uniform ground covering will be achieved.

4 Boxwood is a popular choice for edging. Make a neat hole for each plant and firm some extra soil around them as you go. Maintain an even spacing between the plants because this will help to achieve the formal appearance of your parterre.

5 Once the boxwood or other edging plants are in place, the herbs can be planted. Allocate a specific herb to each section of the parterre or follow a theme.

Once the boxwood hedging has settled and started to fill out, it can be trimmed to shape as desired. Wait until the risk of frost is over in early summer before using a hedge trimmer or edging shears to trim back the new growth.

Chickens

Keeping chickens is a wonderfully rewarding hobby
and will supply you with delicious fresh eggs most days.
Before committing to chickens, however, you need to
make sure that you can visit the garden at least twice a day
to feed and water them, and to close them in at night.

Keeping chickens

When you are working down in the garden, let the chickens out of
their run and allow them to peck over vegetable beds that have
been harvested. They are fantastic at weeding, devouring small
pests, and lightly scratching up the soil. One of the other benefits
of keeping chickens is that they will
give you a regular supply of chicken
manure, which makes a wonderful
soil improver. Make sure it is well
rotted down before adding it to
the soil, since its rich qualities
will burn plant roots. Some
neighborhoods don't allow chickens
to be kept on site, so check before
purchasing them.

Sheltered home Chickens need
a sheltered building with a perch
to sit on. Their run should be as
large as possible and fox-proof.

Chicken breeds There are many
breeds to choose from. Seek advice
for the one that meets your needs
and also suits your conditions.

Chicken houses

Chicken houses come in all sorts
of shapes and sizes, and there are
no hard-and-fast rules regarding
the perfect home. However, they
need to be watertight and
fox-proof, and they must have
a perch inside, since chickens
like to sit high up on a bar
rather than sitting on the floor.
A chicken house also needs
a separate nest area where
the hens can lay their eggs. If
your hens feel safe and happy,
they will lay more eggs.

Bees

Keeping a hive or two of bees is not to everyone's taste. However, if you become a beekeeper, not only will you have a constant supply of your own honey, but the bees will pollinate your flowers, ensuring that you have bigger fruit and vegetable crops.

Buying bees

When you are considering buying bees, talk with your neighbors to ensure they are happy to have hives nearby. A promise of a jar or two of honey is usually enough to convince them. Position the entrance to the beehive away from the neighbor's yard so that nobody accidentally gets stung because they are in the flight path. Before buying your bees, take a short training course to learn the basics. Local beekeeping groups may have evening courses to get you up and running.

Flowers Surround your hive with a range of flowering plants that will encourage bees and other pollinating insects to visit.

"Encourage bees to your plot."

Homemade Bumblebees and solitary bees will pollinate your plants. Encourage them to live in your garden by providing them with homemade homes.

Honey

Honey is made from the nectar collected by bees from the surrounding area. Although they will travel quite far in search of suitable plants, they would much rather forage closer to home, so choose a range of plants that will flower for as much of the year as possible. Bees will even forage during winter if the weather is mild enough. The honey will be a distillation of your fruit and vegetable beds in a jar. Perfect!

crop rotation

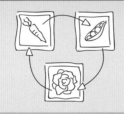

soil **fertility** • **three- & four-year** rotation • catch crops
• **interplanting** •
catch crop partners
• **interplanting** partners

step 9

Crop rotation

When considering planting or sowing your first vegetables, it is a good idea to have a long-term plan. A basic understanding of where to plant your crops over the next three or four years is important for maximizing the space available and caring for the fertility of your soil.

The concept of crop rotation

This essential gardening technique can seem daunting and rather confusing at first, but it is actually a very simple concept. The idea is that annual crops are grown in a different section of the vegetable patch each year. By doing this, it avoids the problem of pests and diseases building up in the soil, which can happen if crops are grown in the same location two years running or more. For the purposes of crop rotation, the hundreds of vegetable crops have been categorized into three, or sometimes four, basic groups: root and potato crops, the cabbage family (or brassicas), and the pea and bean family (or legumes). So, in order to rotate the crops, in the second year the crops in Bed 1 go to Bed 3; those in Bed 3 go to Bed 2; and Bed 2 crops go to Bed 1 (see right).

Three-year rotation

Most people operate a three-year crop rotation program, because it is the simplest to manage. On a really small plot you can operate just two groups, which could be potatoes grouped with root crops, rotated with everything else. Some crops, such as pumpkins, lettuce, and zucchini, suffer from fewer diseases and can be planted wherever there is space.

- Year 1: potatoes, tomatoes, and root crops
- Year 2: peas and beans
- Year 3: cabbage family

Four-year rotation

For more advanced planning, a four-year crop rotation can be used, separating potatoes and tomatoes from root vegetables. Sadly, blight, which affects them both, is airborne, and crop rotation won't prevent it.

- Year 1: potatoes and tomatoes
- Year 2: root vegetables
- Year 3: peas and beans
- Year 4: cabbage family

Benefits of rotation

One of the benefits of crop rotation is that it maximizes the amount of fertility available in the soil for specific groups of vegetables. For example, peas and beans fix nitrogen in the soil, so it makes sense to plant cabbage after peas and beans, since the cabbage's leafy growth thrives in nitrogen-rich soil. Similarly, peas like a deep soil, so plant those after your root crops have loosened the ground and broken up the soil somewhat.

Avoiding fresh manure Carrots don't appreciate growing in a freshly manured bed, so it is best to plant them after the cabbage group.

Pests and diseases Moving the crops each year prevents a buildup of diseases in the soil, but won't prevent slugs, snails, and flying pests.

Control of weeds Use potatoes for the first year of crop rotation—they help to break up the soil and should help to smother some weeds.

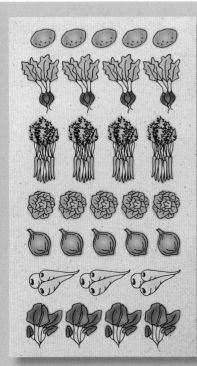

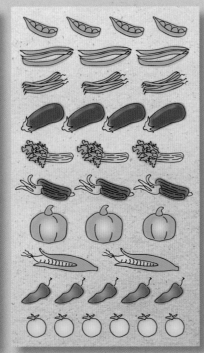

Bed 1 Potatoes and root vegetables are usually planted first, because this breaks up the soil and creates a nice deep root run for the crops that will follow them.

Bed 2 Peas and beans are legumes and store nitrogen in their root nodules. They are planted after the root vegetables and thrive in the deep soil vacated by root crops.

Bed 3 The cabbage family includes Brussels sprouts, broccoli, cauliflower, cabbage, and kale. These crops will thrive in the nitrogen-rich soil left by the legumes.

Don't rotate

Crop rotation is only for annual plants since perennials stay where they have been planted for a few years. This means that you do not have to include plants such as rhubarb, asparagus, perennial herbs, and fruit trees or bushes in your crop-rotation plans. However, their long-term location should be considered when planning which crops are going where.

Asparagus These delicious spears are usually grown in their own section of the garden. Make sure the site is thoroughly prepared prior to planting, because they will be in the ground for a few years.

Rhubarb These colorful, leafy plants can get extremely large and will need quite a lot of space to grow to their full potential. Use them to fill those tricky shady corners, where they will thrive.

Fruit trees and bushes When planning the garden, it is a good idea to get the fruiting plants in first; they will form the structure of your garden and other plants can be worked around them.

Catch cropping & interplanting

step 9

Once you have worked out where your main crops are to go, you can turn your attention to growing catch crops and interplanting. These are good ways to maximize your space and benefit from some quick-result crops as a bonus.

Catch crops

This is a popular technique that involves sowing quick-growing crops in the bare soil between your larger, slower-growing crops before the slower crops reach full maturity. For example, you could sow some fast-growing salad greens between your widely spaced, slower-growing cauliflower heads. However, it is important to remember to harvest the fast-growing crops before they start to compete with the hungry larger plants for the nutrients in the soil.

Catch crop partners

Small, fast-growing crops include radishes, beet tops, arugula, salad greens, and spinach. Large, slower-growing crops are usually from the cabbage family. When planting main-crop plants, leave some extra space to allow room for catch crops in between.

PARTNERS

- Brussels sprouts with radishes
- cauliflower with lettuce
- cabbage with baby carrots
- kale with baby beets
- broccoli with baby turnip tops

Project Sweet corn

Sweet corn provides shade for the lettuce so the two crops are perfect parners.

Sprinkle seed over the surface and water it using a can with a fine nozzle.

step 1

1   Being a wind-pollinated plant, sweet corn should be grown in a grid rather than in rows. Use a stick to mark out the grid pattern.

step 2

2   Dig planting holes 18in (45cm) apart with a trowel, following your marked-out grid pattern, then plant the sweet corn seedlings.

step 3

3   Scatter lettuce seed in between the sweet corn. After germination, thin out the seedlings to give space for the lettuce to grow.

"Sow quick-growing crops after the main crop has been harvested."

Catch cropping

Interplanting

This is similar to growing catch crops, but rather than sowing between slow-growing crops, you sow quick-growing crops after a main crop has been harvested but before another crop is ready to go in the ground. For example, your plan is to dig up early-grown fava beans in spring and replace them with Brussels sprouts. If the sprouts seedlings aren't yet ready, you can sow and harvest another quick-growing crop while you're waiting for them. The bonus is that you utilize space that might otherwise turn into a weed patch. Fast-growing crops include lettuce, radishes, and spinach. Or try green manures such as mustard, heliotrope, red clover, or lupines. Most will add nitrogen to the soil as well as preventing weeds.

Interplanting

Space savers This is a good example of catch cropping—fast-growing lettuce planted between slower-growing sweet corn.

Interplanting partners

Salads, leafy crops, and radishes are best for fast-growing interplanting vegetables. Always keep an eye out for space so you can maximize the amount of produce you get from your garden. Sowing seeds every few weeks will mean you have a regular supply of vegetables. Combined with the use of cloches during cooler periods, interplanting should ensure you have vegetables all year long, with no gaps between harvesting one crop and waiting for the next one to grow. If you still have patches of bare soil, cover them with weed barrier to keep them clear.

PARTNERS

- early peas—radishes—fall turnips
- parsnips (harvested by early spring)—salad greens—string beans
- fava beans—spinach—leeks

step 10

sowing & planting

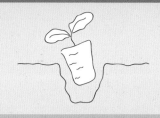

sowing seeds indoors •
sowing methods • sowing seeds
outside • planting methods
• fruit trees & bushes

step 10

Starting plants inside

You will start most plants off by sowing seeds. One exception is garlic, where you plant a clove. The start of the growing season is exciting, and it's a feeling that never wanes, however many years you plant it. If you have limited space, don't waste it by sowing seeds that germinate well outdoors. Instead, use it for tender crops, such as bell peppers and tomatoes, that require a long growing season.

Sideways on Zucchini, squash, and pumpkin seeds should be sown in spring on their side to prevent water from setting on the surface and rotting them.

Garlic cloves Plant these indoors in winter or spring by pushing cloves firmly into the soil mix, leaving just the tip above the surface. Keep well watered and plant outside in early spring.

Sowing methods

There are various techniques for sowing seeds indoors. Much depends on the size of seed and the container that is used. As a rule of thumb, large seeds, such as cucumbers, fava beans, and pumpkins, are sown individually into pots, since they need the space to grow. Medium-sized seeds are often sown into cells, with one or two seeds in each one. Small seeds, such as lettuce and leeks, are often scattered onto a seed flat and pricked out, or moved into individual pots later. Some pot-sown seeds are potted on—moved to larger pots—before they are planted out. Certain vegetables are nearly always grown directly outdoors since they don't transfer well. The taproots of carrots, for instance, don't like disturbance, while potatoes are too large to be transferred. However, potatoes do benefit from being started indoors first (see Potatoes, p.152), but are then planted directly in the soil.

Bell peppers are rather tender and need a long growing season, so they need sowing indoors in early spring into individual pots. Plant them out in spring after the risk of frost is over.

Chile seeds are fairly large and will benefit from being sown individually into pots and placed in a propagator at 64°F (18°C). Keep them well watered while they germinate.

Green beans love the deep root run provided by toilet-paper rolls and can be sown individually into each "pot." The cardboard rolls will rot when they are planted outdoors.

Indoor sowing

Sowing your seeds indoors enables you to get your crops off to an early start, extends the growing season, and prevents seedlings from being destroyed by a hard frost.

- ◆ **IDEALLY, SEEDS SHOULD BE SOWN** in a greenhouse or polytunnel. If you don't have either of these, then they can be sown at home and placed on a sunny windowsill. Cheap, heated propagators can be purchased to get your seedlings off to an early start. A temperature of around 54°F (12°C) is required for hardy crops and 64°F (18°C) for the more tender ones.
- ◆ **DON'T FORGET** that plants sown indoors will need hardening off if they are to spend the rest of their days outdoors. Do this by leaving them outside during the day for about a week and bringing them in at night. Alternatively, you can place them in a cold frame for a few days before you plant them outdoors.

How to sow seeds

There are many different techniques for seed sowing. Which to use depends partly on the size of the seed, but also on whether seedlings can cope with root disturbance or close competition from other seedlings growing nearby.

Seeds can also be sown inside or out, although certain crops, particularly root crops, such as carrots, radishes, parsnips, turnips, and beets should always be sown directly. There are few hard and fast rules; these are just suggestions below, but experiment to see what works best for you. All a seed really needs is soil or potting mix, light, and water.

HOW MANY SEEDS

- **One seed per pot:** fava beans, globe artichokes, celery root
- **A few seeds per pot:** cauliflower, Florence fennel, tomatoes, green onions, onions
- **Two seeds per pot:** green beans, string beans
- **In a long tube (such as a toilet-paper roll):** sweet peas, peas, snow peas, sweet corn
- **A few seeds in cell packs:** Brussels sprouts, kohlrabi, broccoli
- **In a seed flat:** leeks, cabbage, lettuce, celery (on the surface)
- **On their sides:** zucchini, cucumbers, pumpkins, squash
- **In a heated propagator:** chiles, melons, tomatoes, peppers, eggplant

Cabbage has medium-sized seeds and should be sown with one or two seeds per cell into seed-starting mix. Thin the seedlings out to one per cell once they have germinated.

Brussels sprouts should be sown into cell packs and then pricked out into larger pots when they have germinated. Firm the soil thoroughly after planting out.

Fava beans can be sown one seed per pot or "growing tube" in late fall for an early crop the following year. In warmer areas you can sow them directly outdoors in fall or spring.

step 10 Starting plants outside

Most vegetables can be sown directly outdoors, so if you don't have a greenhouse or room on your window ledge to nurse your emerging seedlings under cover, it doesn't matter. You may have to wait until a little later in the year before sowing some of the more tender plants outside—just check the seed packets.

Preparing for seed sowing

Break up the soil in the vegetable bed and add plenty of bulky organic material, such as garden compost or well-rotted manure. Dig over the bed, removing any weeds or rocks. Then rake over the soil to produce a fine tilth, or fine crumbly soil, because a far finer grade of soil is needed for sowing than for planting. Avoid adding fresh manure or compost if sowing carrots.

Get ready Dig in a lot of organic matter and rake it level. Ideally, leave the soil to settle before sowing.

Sowing methods

Small seeds such as carrots, lettuce, and parsnips are usually sown thinly in furrows in the soil. Furrows can be made by using the edge of a hoe along the line created by a string tied tightly between two stakes, ensuring that the furrow is truly straight. Seeds germinate better if the furrow is moistened lightly before sowing, using a watering can with a fine nozzle. Larger seeds are usually sown directly at their final spacing. Often a cluster of seeds can be sown at each spot and thinned out to the strongest seedling. Larger seeds are sown using a dibber, or pointed wooden stick, to create the hole. The seed is placed in the hole, which is then backfilled and watered. Occasionally, seed beds are created by scattering seeds over a prepared area, raking them in, and pricking them out later into their final locations. This is often the technique used for sowing leeks. Protect all your seedlings from slugs and snails.

Beans of all types are hungry plants, so add plenty of organic matter prior to sowing. Sow two or three seeds in each hole. Thin the seedlings out to the strongest when they emerge.

Zucchini are usually sown indoors but they can be sown outside after the risk of frost is over. They like heavy soil, so add lots of organic matter to the ground before sowing.

Pumpkins should be sown with two or three seeds in each hole, thinned out to the strongest after germination. Put plenty of well-rotted manure around each seedling.

Direct sowing

Sowing outdoors, otherwise known as direct sowing, is easy. You can warm the seed bed up first by covering it with plastic sheeting or by placing cloches over it for a few days prior to sowing. This will help to speed up the process of germination. Always have a sheet of row cover or a cloche ready later on if it looks as if the emerging seedlings are going to get hit by frost.

◆ **EMERGING SEEDLINGS** often need to be thinned out to the strongest and healthiest plants. Information about the space you should leave between seedlings when thinning them is provided on the back of the seed packet. Keep the area free from competing weeds and water the plants regularly as they grow.

If you wish to continue sowing and harvesting vegetables into fall and winter, the plants will need to be covered up with cloches or row cover to protect them from the cold.

How to sow your seeds outside

Many of the seeds listed below can be sown indoors in flats and pots as well as outdoors. This is a general guide; some varieties are dwarfing or more vigorous, so adjust their spacing accordingly. Nor are the distances given final, since many seeds are later thinned out. Always check planting distances on the back of seed packets and if in doubt, ask an experienced gardener. A bonus of working in your vegetable garden is that nearby neighbors will be able to offer friendly advice and you can benefit from their experience.

- **Sow thinly in a furrow:** broccoli, Brussels sprouts, cabbage, cauliflower, kale, beets, carrots, turnips, spinach, rutabagas, lettuce, radishes
- **Sow 4in (10cm) apart:** garlic sets, onion sets
- **Sow 6in (15cm) apart:** string beans, green beans
- **Sow 12–15in (30–38cm) apart:** perpetual spinach
- **Plant in blocks:** leeks, sweet corn
- **Plant in a flat furrow:** peas 2–2¾in (5–7cm) apart in staggered rows, Swiss chard
- **Plant in staggered rows 9in (23cm) apart:** fava beans
- **Plant in a seed bed for transplanting later:** leeks (thinly) in drills 6in (15cm) apart and ¼in (1cm) deep
- **Sow two seeds in pairs 3ft (90cm) apart:** zucchini, large squashes
- **Sow two seeds in pairs 5ft (1.5m) apart:** pumpkins, squashes
- **Tubers:** potatoes (early) 12in (30cm) apart, potatoes (main) 16–30in (40–75cm), Jerusalem artichokes 3ft (90cm) apart.

Cabbage should be sown sparingly and thinned regularly as they grow to a final spacing of about 12–18in (30–45cm). If the soil is acidic, it should have lime added to it first.

Lettuce should be sown thinly in shallow furrows. It can be cut as young leaves or thinned out to grow bigger plants. Sow seeds every two weeks for crops throughout the season.

Potatoes are planted in spring into rows of trenches, then covered with soil enriched with organic matter. Gently mound the soil up as the young plant shoots emerge.

Planting methods

Sweet corn Being a wind-pollinated plant, sweet corn should be planted not in rows, but in a grid pattern to aid pollination.

> "use a wooden **board** to walk on **beds**."

There are many different techniques for planting your crops. It all depends on whether you are planting out your seedlings or planting young fruit trees and bushes. Whichever it is, your two main requirements are well-prepared soil and regular watering after planting.

Planting vegetable seedlings

You can either grow seedlings yourself or buy them at your local garden center. Although it is more expensive to buy ready-grown plants, it is a useful time saver if you haven't had a chance to grow everything you want from seed. Always check the labels on packets of seeds and plants, since planting requirements—and especially the recommended distances between plants—vary for each type of vegetable. Even within a group of plants such as cabbage, the distance between each one can range from 12in (30cm) for compact types to 18in (45cm) for larger varieties. When you are planting out, use a wooden board to walk over the vegetable beds to prevent your shoes from compacting the soil.

Planting methods

Top-heavy plants such as sweet corn and Brussels sprouts benefit from having the soil firmed around their roots to stop them from blowing over in the wind. Certain other plants such as leeks shouldn't be firmed in at all; this leaves room for their stems to expand and widen. If planting in rows, use string tied between stakes to ensure you plant in straight lines. Most vegetables should be planted with the top of their roots flush with the soil.

Cabbage These should be planted firmly into rich, fertile soil. Always check the label for planting distances.

Leeks These are planted differently to most other crops. Use a large dibber, or pointed wooden stick, to create a hole and pop the seedling into it. Don't firm down the soil around it, but instead water it in, leaving the soil to crumble back around the leek.

Keep weeds at bay After planting a fruit tree, suppress weeds by applying weed barrier or a layer of mulch around the roots.

Planting fruit trees & bushes

When planting young trees, attach them to a stake to help them grow straight and prevent them from being blown over. Put the stake in the soil before the tree to prevent damage to the roots. Alternatively, use a diagonal stake at 45 degrees.

◆ **USE A TREE GUARD** around the trunk if rabbits are a problem.

◆ **FRUIT TREES** grown on dwarf rootstocks (the rootstock is the lower trunk and roots, onto which a tree is grafted—it can dictate tree size and disease-resistance) are a good choice. Such trees will not grow too big, will not create too much shade, and their roots will not grow into your vegetable beds.

◆ **BARE-ROOT FRUIT TREES** are usually available from late fall through to late winter. They are often cheaper and healthier than container-grown trees. Bare-root trees should be planted while still dormant; container trees can be planted at nearly any time of year.

Planting depths

Do not plant fruit trees too deeply—this can quickly rot the trunk. Most trees have a graft union low down on the trunk, where the tree has been grafted onto a rootstock (see left). The graft union should always remain above the soil.

Apple Place a stick across the hole to check the tree is at the same level as it was in its pot. Backfill with quality potting mix.

Black currants Black currants are an exception; plant them about 2in (5cm) deeper than they were in their pot.

Raspberries These are planted out as individual canes. Plant them to the same depth as the soil mark on the canes.

Containers

Fruit trees and bushes can be grown in containers. This is ideal if the soil in the garden is poor. It also restricts the size of the tree, preventing it from getting too big for the yard. Choose dwarf varieties of fruit trees for pots and containers.

Potting mix and fertilizer Ensure the container has adequate drainage and combine potting mix and fertilizer.

Level of soil Plant the tree at the same depth as it was in its pot and firm it in well. Mulch the surface with compost.

First season The center of the garden has been cleared and all the projects completed. There is a lovely seating area, and the raised beds and herb parterre contain flourishing crops, some of which are ready to harvest. The whole area is protected by rabbit-proof fencing, and the plot now has a clear structure, which can be developed in future seasons.

VEGETABLES

Growing & Storing

vegetables

leafy crops

cabbage & Asian brassicas • Brussels sprouts • spinach & chard • lettuce & salad greens • chicory & endive • kale

Cabbage & Asian brassicas

Not only is cabbage healthy and surprisingly tasty, but it also has a wonderful ornamental quality to it, coming in a wide range of shapes and colors and adding interest and texture to the kitchen garden. But the main reason it is so useful is that it will provide a bumper crop nearly all year round.

Netting Net cabbageheads to protect them from cabbage white butterflies and birds.

Sowing

Sow cabbage seeds from early spring to late summer, depending on their group (see right). You can either sow them under cover in small plastic pots or in a seed bed.

Transplanting When the plants are 2½in (6cm) tall, transplant them to their final location, leaving 12–18in (30–45cm) between each plant.

Growing

Cabbage fall into three groups—spring, summer, and winter, depending on when they are to be harvested. Spring cabbage is sown in July and August and transplanted in September/October. Summer cabbage is sown from early March until early May and transplanted in May/June. Winter cabbage is sown in April/May, then transplanted in late June/July. Firm transplanted cabbage in well to prevent the wind from rocking them.

◆ **CABBAGE REQUIRES** a sunny, sheltered location in rich, fertile but well-drained soil. Dig in organic matter such as well-rotted manure before planting. If your soil is poor, consider building raised beds and filling them with a mix of good-quality soil, potting mix, and manure. Avoid growing cabbage in the same area as the previous year since they are prone to soilborne diseases such as clubroot. Instead, practice crop rotation.

savoy

smooth cabbage

pointed cabbage

Asian greens

These late-summer vegetables can be eaten raw, added to stir-fries, or cooked like traditional cabbage. They require fertile soil in full sun. Sow seeds in furrows ½in (1cm) deep in rows 15in (38cm) apart. Thin seedlings to 6in (15cm) apart for cut-and-come-again salad greens or 12in (30cm) apart for large heads.

Mulching Regularly water and mulch Chinese cabbage lettuce to prevent plants from bolting.

Cut leaves Harvest succulent young leaves with scissors as a cut-and-come-again crop.

Harvest whole Alternatively, leave plants to form large heads and harvest at the end of summer.

Routine care

Cabbage are hungry plants so give them a liquid fertilizer every couple of weeks to keep them lush and healthy. Water them daily during dry periods and weed around the plants regularly to keep them from having to compete with the weeds for nutrients.

◆ **WATCH OUT** for pests and diseases. The worst culprits are birds—they will tear cabbageheads to shreds, so cover the heads with a net. Cabbage white butterflies and cabbage maggots are the other pests to watch out for (see p.127).

Harvesting Spring cabbage is ready to harvest during April and May, summer cabbage between July and September, and fall and winter cabbage from September onward.

Storing & Using

Cabbage can be used for: salads...stir-fries...soups... sauerkraut...casseroles...

Cabbages can remain in the ground for longer than many other vegetables so you can cut them and use them as and when you want. If you want to store them, the traditional method is to put them in a net in a cool, dry garage or cellar.

Sauerkraut This traditional dish uses very finely shredded cabbage that has been pickled or fermented. It will keep for many months.

red cabbage

Chinese broccoli

bok choy

mizuna

Brussels sprouts

Although not to everybody's taste, Brussels sprouts are rich in vitamin C, and there are lots of tasty ways of cooking them to give them wider appeal. A useful crop for winter use, new varieties have been bred for extra sweetness, and there are also exciting red-leaved varieties to try.

Acquired taste Brussels sprouts are sweet and tender when young, and become even sweeter and more delicious once they have been touched by frost a few times.

Sowing outdoors

Plants can either be sown under cover and then planted out as seedlings (see below), or sown directly into the soil in spring.

◆ **IF SOWING** directly into the ground, the soil should be thoroughly dug over and all weeds removed. Like other members of the cabbage family, Brussels sprouts prefer a heavy, rich soil, so add lots of organic matter, such as well-rotted manure. Rake the soil level then let it settle for a couple of weeks before sowing.

◆ **SOW SEED** in mid-spring. Use the edge of a hoe to create a shallow ½in (1cm) furrow, or narrow trench, in the soil and sow thinly in rows 6in (15cm) apart. When the seedlings emerge, they should be thinned out to 3in (7.5cm).

Sowing indoors

Seeds can be sown indoors in late winter for an early crop in late summer. Fill cell packs with good-quality seed-starting mix and water well. Use a dibber to make a ¾in (2cm) hole in each cell and sow two seeds. Water again and then leave to germinate. Thin out to leave the strongest seedling in each cell. As with all seedlings, harden them off for 7–10 days before planting them outside.

Strongest seedlings Select the strongest and healthiest seedlings to plant out when they have reached 4in (10cm) tall.

Planting distance Seedlings should be planted 24in (60cm) apart. Firm them in well after planting and water thoroughly.

Cabbage collar Plants are prone to damage by cabbage maggots. Place cabbage collars at the base of the stems.

Routine care

Keep the plants well watered during dry periods, and mulch around the base of the plants with well-rotted manure to retain moisture. Brussels sprouts are tall plants and may need support using stakes and string in exposed, windy sites.

◆ **MOST OLDER** varieties ripen upward from the bottom of the stem. Newer varieties develop at a more equal rate and can be cut as whole stems once all the sprouts reach a good size.

◆ **SPROUTS CAN** either be removed from the stem with a sharp knife or twisted off with your fingers. Harvest as and when they are needed—they don't keep for long after picking.

Harvesting Brussels sprouts sown in fall are ready for harvesting from winter to spring. Plants sown indoors in winter will be ready to harvest in late summer.

Storing & Using

They can be used in: soups... stir-fries...or mashed... or frozen...

Brussels sprouts are best picked as you need them. They can also be kept in the refrigerator for a week, or blanch them and keep in a freezer for about 12 months. Brussels sprouts mean Christmas dinner to many people, but they can be used in many ways. Their flavor goes well with many things: blue cheese, bacon, or sour cream. Tossed with butter and Parmesan cheese, they make a tasty side dish.

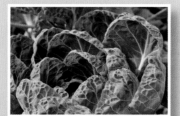

Sprout tops These bushy leaves at the top of the stalk are less pungent than sprouts but extremely tender, and can be used like kale or cabbage.

sprouts

Growing tips

Brussels sprouts are easy to grow, but watch out for some of the pests that all members of the cabbage family are prone to, such as cabbage maggots, cabbage white butterflies, and birds.

Netting Cover plants with netting to prevent the crop from being damaged by birds. Pigeons are particularly fond of the leaves of Brussels sprouts.

Hilling up Prevent these top-heavy vegetables from toppling in the wind by hilling soil up around the base of each plant for extra stability.

Good practice Remove the aging yellow leaves as the plant matures to improve air circulation and prevent the sprouts from rotting.

Spinach & Chard

Fresh spinach leaves are so tasty and healthy to eat that it's no wonder Popeye was such a devotee. They can be regularly harvested while young and used in salads, or left to mature for cooking. Chard leaves are also delicious, with the bonus that they add a splash of color to the garden with their vivid stems.

Cold protection Protect early-sown crops with a cloche, but remove for a time on warm days.

Sowing

Sow chard in mid-spring. Make a 1in (2.5cm) furrow and sow seeds about 3in (7.5cm) apart, in rows spaced at 15in (38cm). Water the rows well and label the plants.

Sow seeds individually Sow spinach seeds 1in (2.5cm) apart from early spring to early summer, in furrows ½in (1cm) deep. Cover over with soil and water thoroughly.

Thinning Seedlings can be thinned out when they are ¾in (2cm) tall. Chard should be thinned to 12in (30cm) apart, spinach to 8in (20cm) apart.

Growing

Both spinach and chard prefer a sunny or slightly shaded location in moist but free-draining soil. Both are easy to grow, although they have slightly different sowing and harvesting times.

- ◆ **CHARD SHOULD** be sown mainly in springtime, directly into the soil, which will give a regular crop of attractive leaves during the summer months. It is possible to extend the season through to fall or winter with later sowings and by keeping the plants protected under cloches.

- ◆ **SPINACH IS** either sown outside in spring and harvested in early summer, or sown in late summer and harvested in fall. In order to guarantee a constant supply of spinach, you can sow seed every two to three weeks.

spinach

white chard

Routine care

Both spinach and chard require relatively little upkeep once sown and thinned. Look out for mildew on spinach and remove affected leaves. Choose varieties that offer disease resistance. Keep the seedlings free of weeds and water the plants regularly during dry spells. Give the plants a high-nitrogen liquid fertilizer every couple of weeks to keep them green and productive.

◆ **IF YOU WISH** to grow spinach as a cut-and-come-again crop, don't thin out the seedlings and harvest the leaves regularly.

Harvesting

Spring sowings of chard are ready for harvesting about 12 weeks after sowing, while spinach can be cut after 8–12 weeks. Pick sooner if growing them as cut-and-come-again.

Young shoots Regularly pick the leaves to ensure that new fresh growth is produced. Leaves can be harvested young, as soon as they are large enough, or left to reach full size. Take care not to damage the main growing point in the center.

Harvesting all If preferred, you can harvest whole plants all at once, leaving room for others nearby to develop.

Bolting Keep chard plants well watered during summer to prevent them from flowering—or bolting—which spoils the crop. Spinach has a tendency to bolt, particularly in hot, dry weather. Choose resistant varieties or grow in light shade.

Storing & Using

They can be made into: soups...salads...casseroles ...quiches...or frozen...

Spinach and chard leaves taste best when picked young and fresh, and can be added to salads. Brightly colored chard stems are also edible and can be used in a range of dishes. Spinach and chard can both be frozen. Blanch first by boiling for a couple of minutes, cooling in iced water, then drying on a dish towel. Once frozen, both are best when cooked rather than eaten raw or in salads.

rhubarb chard

rainbow chard

red chard

Lettuce & Salad greens

Lettuce is often the main ingredient used in salads, and the range of varieties is extensive. However, it is only one of many leafy salad crops, which include tasty arugula, sorrel, and corn salad. Salad greens are quick and easy to grow, which also makes them perfect "fillers" for squeezing in between slower growing crops, such as turnips. With a bit of planning and cold protection, it is possible to be harvesting salad greens nearly all year.

Sowing outdoors

Salad greens can be sown outdoors in furrows from early spring to late summer. Dig over the soil, removing any weeds, before raking the area so the surface is level.

Make a furrow Draw out a furrow about ½in (1cm) deep and then lightly sow the seeds, cover them over with soil, and then water them lightly.

Thinning out Plants grown for mature, full-sized heads should be thinned out to about 10in (25cm) apart. Don't thin cut-and-come-again crops.

Growing

There are basically four types of lettuce. Romaine types are upright with loose hearts. Head lettuces have tightly folded, crunchy leaves and a solid heart, such as iceberg. Butter has soft, folded leaves with round hearts. Finally, there are the looseleaf types, which can be grown as cut-and-come-again. Lettuce prefers light, well-drained soil, and will tolerate some light shade. It is a good choice for growing in containers if kept well watered.

◆ **SEEDS CAN BE** sown directly in the soil (see left) or, for an earlier crop, they can also be sown in late winter under cover and planted out when the risk of cold has passed.

◆ **WHEN SOWING UNDER COVER**, sow two or three seeds into small pots of potting mix. Thin to leave the biggest seedling.

◆ **KEEP PLANTS** well watered during dry periods, since this will help prevent bolting, or running to seed. Regularly weed among the growing plants to prevent any competition for nutrients.

'Little Gem'

'Tom Thumb'

'Lollo Rosso'

Protection

Slugs and snails can swiftly devastate a healthy crop of salad greens, particularly during wet weather. Protect plants by laying grit or sharp sand around them, or lightly sprinkle slug pellets around the area. Aphids also enjoy feeding on leaves, so check over the plants regularly.

Grit Sprinkle grit or sharp sand around the plants because slugs hate the coarse, dry texture.

Netting If birds are a problem in your garden, cover lettuce plants with a net to protect them.

Plastic bottles Use plastic bottles to protect leaves from slugs. They also act as mini cloches.

Harvesting

Cut-and-come-again crops are simply cut just above the base of the plants using scissors once the leaves are large enough. They will then resprout, ready to crop again in a few days if watered well. Cut regularly to keep the leaves from getting too leggy.

◆ **HEARTING TYPES**, those that form heads, should be cut just above the soil using a sharp knife.

◆ **LOOSELEAF VARIETIES** are best harvested only when required, because they soon wilt. The cut leaves will keep in the refrigerator for a day or two.

Pick again Pick and sow seeds frequently for a regular supply of lettuce for your salad bowl.

corn salad

arugula

Batavia

romaine

sorrel

Chinese

Chicory & Endive

These crops are grown in a similar way to lettuce, although they are hardier and can be harvested well into fall. There are three types of chicory: sugar loaf, red-leaved (or radicchio), and Witloof. There are also two different types of endive: curly-leaved varieties and Belgian types, which have broad leaves.

Belgian endive

Sowing

Chicory and endive can be sown indoors for a head start, or outside a few weeks later. Wait until the soil has started to warm if sowing outside to keep the plants from bolting.

Sowing seeds Dig over the site, remove any weeds, and sow thinly into furrows, ½in (1cm) deep.

Watering Thin seedlings out to 12in (30cm) apart and keep them well watered throughout summer.

Witloof chicory

Growing

Chicory and endive require rich, well-drained soil, and will grow in sun or light shade. Winter crops can be grown under cover or in cloches.

◆ **SOW SEEDS** under cover in early spring; directly outside from mid-spring.

◆ **PLANTS SHOULD** be kept well watered during summer to prevent them from bolting.

◆ **ENDIVE CAN** be blanched to reduce bitterness by tying the leaves together and placing a pot over them. Harvest the head after 15 days.

curly endive

◆ **PICK WHEN** leaves have reached a suitable size. Baby leaves can also be harvested as required, as cut-and-come-again salad greens.

"Chicons" Witloof chicory is often forced to produce "chicons," or fleshy shoots, in winter. Plant mature roots into pots in fall and keep them dark. Harvest the shoots when 4in (10cm) tall.

radicchio

Kale

These vitamin-rich plants are one of the most ornamental and architectural members of the cabbage family, with a range of different shapes, heights, and colors, including varieties with crinkly and curly leaves, and colored foliage.

Growing

Kale requires rich, fertile, but well-drained soil, and plenty of space, although dwarf varieties are available. Young plants are planted out or transplanted in early summer into their final locations. Stake taller varieties to keep them from blowing over.

◆ **PROTECT KALE** from cabbage maggots by placing collars around the base of each plant. Cover with a fine-meshed net to keep cabbage white butterflies and pigeons from attacking them.

◆ **LEAVES CAN** be harvested throughout fall and winter by picking them individually. Dispose of the plants when they flower the following spring.

Harvesting Harvest the tender inner leaves every few days. The outer leaves are coarser and less tasty.

Sowing

Seeds can be sown ½in (1cm) deep into pots under cover in spring, or directly into rows outside from mid-spring. Plants raised outside are transplanted into their final locations once large enough.

Indoor seedlings Seedlings raised indoors should be grown until large enough to plant outside in their final locations. Repot them as required.

Planting distance Plants should be planted out, spaced 18in (45cm) apart. Keep them well watered and support taller varieties as they grow.

Storing & Using

It can be used in: quiches... soups...or can be frozen...

Kale goes well with fish and meat, and is commonly boiled or steamed to accompany beef dishes. It can also be used in stir-fries, casseroles, and pasta dishes. Refrigerate the leaves for up to a week or freeze them for up to 9 months.

Pie Using either pie crust or filo pastry, kale can be combined with cheese, onions, and eggs to make a tasty pie.

purple kale

green kale

vegetables
fruiting & flowering

tomatoes • cucumbers & eggplant • broccoli & cauliflower • zucchini & summer squash • pumpkins • squash • bell peppers & chiles • sweet corn • globe artichokes

Tomatoes

Tomatoes are very easy to grow, either under cover or outside in a sunny location, and produce a reliable harvest from midsummer. There are many varieties to choose from, producing fruit in a wide range of colors, flavors, and sizes. These fall into two types: indeterminate tomatoes that are usually trained up tall stakes or strings, and bush varieties that are grown freely.

Growing bags

Growing bags can be used for tomatoes and allow you to easily give them the sunny, sheltered site they require.

Make a hole The planting holes in your growing bag should be large enough to plant the tomatoes into and to allow easy watering. Remember to make drainage holes in the base.

Keep watered Tomato plants are particularly thirsty when they are in flower or fruit. The potting mix in the growing bags needs to be kept moist.

Growing

Sow tomato seeds under cover in early spring.
Fill a pot or flat with potting mix, water well, and sow the seeds on top, spacing them ½in (1cm) apart. Lightly cover with mix and place in a propagator or on a warm windowsill.

◆ **WHEN THE** seedlings have their first pair of leaves, prick them out into individual pots and grow under cover until the risk of cold has passed. Repot them into larger pots as necessary.

◆ **PLANT OUT** about 12in (30cm) apart, or three per growing bag, in a sheltered but sunny spot. Insert tall stakes near each plant for support—one per indeterminate, or four per bush type.

◆ **IMPROVE THE SOIL** before planting tomatoes out with some well-rotted manure mixed into the soil to give the plants a good start. This also helps to stop the plants from drying out.

plum

beefsteak

salad

cherry plum

yellow cherry

red on

Routine care

If you look after tomatoes properly and give them the right growing conditions, they will reward you with a good, steady crop from about July into September, or even October.

◆ **IT IS IMPORTANT** to keep plants well watered, since drying out will affect their growth and may damage the developing fruit. Use a tomato fertilizer weekly once the flowers appear.

◆ **INDETERMINATE** tomatoes are grown as single stems up a stake or string support. Tie them in with soft twine as they grow. Once these plants have formed four or five trusses of flowers, cut off the top of the plants to stop further growth.

◆ **TOMATOES** ripen from midsummer onward. For the best flavor, wait until each fruit is evenly colored. Smaller tomatoes ripen quickly in good weather but larger fruit, such as beefsteak types, can take several days to ripen completely.

Growing tips

Water all plants regularly, even as much as twice a day in very hot weather, and feed them using a high-potassium tomato fertilizer. Avoid letting plants dry out, which can cause the fruit to split and may lead to the nutrient disorder, blossom end rot (see p.235). If growing tomatoes in a greenhouse, ensure plants are well ventilated.

Support Tie in the stems of indeterminate tomatoes to give them support as they become heavy with the growing fruit.

Pinch back Sideshoots of indeterminate tomatoes should be pinched back regularly, but leave those on bush tomatoes to grow. Pinch back carefully with your fingers, supporting the stem with the other hand.

black cherry grape

Storing & Using

They can be used for: ketchup...salsa...soups... sauces...or can be juiced... or oven-dried...

Tomatoes keep well in the refrigerator for a few days but they do not freeze well. Extras can be oven-dried, or preserved in a wide range of dishes, such as salsa or tomato ketchup, or in used in stocks, sauces, and soup bases that can be frozen.

Oven-dried tomatoes Useful in many dishes, pack them into sterilized jars and cover with olive oil. They will keep for up to 6 months stored in a cool pantry.

Sauce Making ketchup is great fun, and you know exactly what ingredients have gone into it. It will keep for around 6 months in sterilized bottles, and goes just as well with burgers and fries as it does with meatloaf or hot dogs.

Chutney Tomatoes really lend themselves to chutney, and you can use either ripe or green tomatoes. Green tomatoes are good to use at the end of the season. Chutney will keep for 6 to 12 months in a pantry.

Cucumbers

Fresh salads wouldn't be the same without cucumber. It is a summer essential. Containing next to no calories and cool, refreshing, and healthy, this member of the cucurbit family is a must for the vegetable plot. If you don't have a greenhouse, then the most suitable type for growing outdoors is the shorter, thicker-skinned cucumber.

Growing

Cucumbers should be sown in early spring since they require a long growing season to ripen their fruit. However, be aware that they don't like fluctuations in temperature during the early stages of germination, so ensure they have constant warmth at the start. Plant them indoors, sowing one seed per 4in (10cm) pot and placing the pots in a propagator. Once they have germinated, keep them under cover until there is no longer any danger of cold.

◆ **OUTDOOR VARIETIES** have male and female flowers and you may need to help with pollination for them to produce fruit. Do this by simply picking a male flower and pushing it into the female flowers.

◆ **MANY INDOOR VARIETIES** only produce female flowers and do not require pollination. If they are pollinated, the cucumbers will be bitter.

Protection Use cloches to protect the young plants from frost. Cloches will also help to speed up fruiting.

outdoor cucumber

cucumber

Growing tips

Growing tips

If you have enough room, cucumbers can be left to scramble and sprawl over the ground. However, if space is at a premium, consider growing them up bamboo stakes or up a commercially built frame.

Frame Whether you use a commercially built frame or construct your own using bamboo poles, you must tie your growing cucumber plants to it.

Harvesting Harvest cucumbers regularly using pruners. This encourages the plant to crop more, and the younger cucumbers will taste better.

Storing & Using

They can be: pickled...

Eat cucumbers as soon as possible since they aren't suitable for refrigerating for long or for freezing. If you have a lot, pick them small and pickle them in vinegar with dill and spices. They will keep for 6 months.

Eggplant

Eggplant are trickier to grow than some vegetables but are well worth the effort. To grow them successfully, you need a greenhouse or a sunny, sheltered spot. Get the conditions right and you will be rewarded with five or six of these quirky-looking vegetables per plant.

'Black Beauty'

'Calliope'

'Thai Green'

'Raja'

Growing

Repotting Plants grown indoors will need repotting. Take care not to disturb the root ball when you do so.

Fill small plastic pots with seed-starting mix in early spring and sow one seed in each. Water them well and place in a heated propagator. Once the seedlings are 2½in (6cm) tall, remove them from the propagator and place them in the greenhouse or on a windowsill to grow them on.

◆ **TO GROW PLANTS OUTDOORS,** first harden the young plants off in a cold frame. Once the risk of frost is over, plant them out in a warm, sheltered location.

◆ **PICK REGULARLY** to encourage more fruiting and use quickly since eggplant don't keep well. Don't leave the fruit on the plant too long: when you pick them, the eggplant should be nice and shiny. If they have become dull, it is because they are overripe.

Growing tips

When the main shoot reaches about 12in (30cm) tall, cut it off or pinch it off to encourage the development of sideshoots. Water plants regularly and give liquid fertilizer once a week to keep them healthy. Eggplant become heavy as they swell, so support the stems with stakes and string.

Support Use soft twine twisted in a figure-eight around the plant and the stake to provide gentle support for the stem.

Storing & Using

Eggplant can be made into: moussaka...ratatouille...

They can only be refrigerated for a few days and can't be frozen, so use them in dishes that can be frozen, such as moussaka.

Broccoli & Cauliflower

These must be two of the most popular and tasty vegetables from the cabbage family. There are several different types of broccoli: purple and white sprouting, and the more common, large, green-headed broccoli. New cauliflower varieties come in exciting colors such as orange, purple, and yellow and offer gardeners the possibility of harvesting close to all year round.

Sowing outdoors

Sow broccoli and spring cauliflowers into ½in (1cm) deep furrows, cover with soil, and water gently. Sow broccoli seed in mid-spring; spring cauliflowers during fall.

Thinning As the plants develop, thin them to their final spacings. Leave 16in (40cm) between broccoli plants; thin spring cauliflowers to 28in (70cm) apart.

Growing

Cauliflowers and broccoli prefer rich, fertile soil, so dig in plenty of well-rotted manure. Prepare the soil thoroughly before sowing or planting, by digging it over and removing any perennial weeds. Broccoli resents root disturbance, so is sown directly in the soil in mid-spring (see left); cauliflowers to harvest in spring are also sown this way during fall. To give summer cauliflowers a head start, sow them under cover in early spring. Fill small pots with potting mix, sow two seeds in each, ½in (1cm) deep, then thin out the seedlings to leave the strongest per pot.

◆ **PLANT OUT** the summer cauliflower plants when they are about 6in (15cm) tall; they will benefit from being hardened off in a cold frame before you plant them out.

◆ **SUMMER VARIETIES** should be planted at 24in (60cm) apart. Water them well after planting.

broccoli

purple sprouting

broccoli 'Romanesco'

Protection

As the plants grow, keep the soil free from weeds to avoid competition for nutrients. Also keep them well watered to prevent the development of fungal diseases such as mildew. The main pests to look out for are birds, particularly pigeons—they can strip leaves; also be vigilant against cabbage root maggots and caterpillars of the cabbage white butterfly.

Cabbage maggots Place a collar at the base to prevent the adult flies from laying eggs there.

Pests Cover plants with a net to keep birds from destroying the crop or butterflies laying their eggs on it.

Sun Tie the leaves together to prevent white-headed cauliflower from turning yellow in the sun.

Harvesting

Broccoli is ready from midsummer to mid-fall. It should be harvested when the flower heads have developed but just before they actually open. Harvest the central stem first, which will then allow sideshoots to develop for picking later. Purple- and white-sprouting broccoli should be regularly picked: that way their season will extend well into fall. To spread out your cauliflower harvest, start cutting when some of them are young.

◆ **DO NOT LEAVE** cauliflower too long before harvesting since the florets separate and will not taste nearly as good.

Storing & Using

They can be used for: salads...soups...gratins...relishes...and frozen...

Cauliflower can be stored for up to three weeks if you harvest them with their roots intact and leave them in a cool, dry place such as a shed. You cannot keep broccoli in the refrigerator for longer than a week. However, if you are faced with excess, the florets of all these vegetables are suitable for freezing. Be sure to blanch them first to preserve their texture and flavor. They will keep for up to a year.

Piccalilli This crunchy relish includes cauliflower florets and gets its lovely bright yellow color from mustard and turmeric. It keeps for up to 6 months.

white-headed cauliflower

cauliflower 'Violet Queen'

Zucchini & Summer squash

Just one or two plants will reward you with bumper crops throughout the summer, so make sure you allocate some space for these essential and nutritious veggies. Although you can grow specific large-fruited, marrow varieties, if you leave zucchini on the vine for long enough, they will rapidly become as big as marrows.

Pollination Tie up the female flower for up to a day after pollination.

Sowing

Zucchini and summer squash are easy to grow. Seeds should be sown indoors in mid- to late spring. Sow one seed per pot, 1¼in (3cm) deep in general-purpose potting mix.

Sideways Lay the seed on its side to prevent it from rotting in the potting mix before it has a chance to germinate.

Outdoors Seeds can be sown outdoors when there is no more risk of frost. Use a dibber and plant two seeds per hole, 1¼in (3cm) deep and 36in (90cm) apart. Thin to one seedling per hole when they emerge.

Growing

Wait until the risk of frost is over before planting out the seedlings. If they have outgrown their pots, they may need repotting into something bigger if the weather conditions are still unsuitable for growing outside. While keeping them indoors, water every few days and give them liquid fertilizer every two weeks to keep them strong and healthy.

◆ **PREPARE THE** ground a few weeks before planting out to give the soil time to settle. Thoroughly dig the soil over and incorporate plenty of well-rotted manure or compost: zucchini and summer squash require a rich, fertile soil to help them cope with their tendency to produce heavy crops.

◆ **USE A TROWEL** to make the planting hole and place them out at 36in (90cm) apart. Water them in thoroughly.

round varieties

zucchini & blossom

Protection

Young seedlings are vulnerable to slugs and snails when they are first planted in the soil, particularly if it has been a damp spring. To combat these pests, lightly sprinkle slug pellets around the area. Alternatively, you can set beer traps or place sharp sand or grit around individual plants. A sprinkling of bran also helps to deter slugs.

Glass panels Place panels of glass around individual plants for the first few days to protect the leaves from cool spring evenings.

Cloches If sowing directly, the soil can be warmed up beforehand by erecting cloches for a few days prior to planting.

Plastic bottles Use old plastic bottles to create mini cloches for seedlings when they are still vulnerable to late-spring frost.

Routine care

Watch out for powdery mildew. Keeping the roots well watered should help prevent it from spreading too quickly. Remove infected leaves as soon as they appear.

♦ **HARVEST** zucchini with pruners or a knife when they reach about 5in (12cm) long. They need to be picked regularly to keep the plants cropping. If you want marrows, leave some to develop further.

Watering If you can't manage to water your plants every day, plunge an upside-down bottle with its end cut off and filled with water into the soil next to the plant. This will keep it watered for a few days.

Storing & Using

They can be used for: stuffing...soups...stews... cakes & muffins...fritters...salads...or frozen...

As well as harvesting squash and eating them right away, you can also use the large, yellow trumpetlike flowers of zucchini to make fritters. Zucchini and summer squash can be frozen (they will keep for about 6 months) but they aren't as tasty once they have been defrosted, so use the defrosted vegetables in delicious soups and sauces, which you can then freeze and use whenever you please.

Muffins Surprisingly, zucchini and summer squash can also successfully be made into delicious muffins and cakes, which bear a resemblance to carrot cake.

marrow 'Tiger Cross'

Pumpkins

Pumpkins are hungry plants and produce their lush foliage and attractive fruit in a rich, heavy soil. If you have poor, infertile soil then you could try growing one on top of the compost heap. Available in a huge variety of shapes, sizes, and colors, pumpkins will make an attractive addition to your kitchen garden.

Growing

Seeds should be sown indoors between mid-April and mid-May, which will give the seedlings a chance to get established before you plant them outside. Fill a 3in (7cm) pot with good-quality seed-starting mix and sow one seed per pot—with the seed on its side to prevent it from rotting—at a depth of 1in (2.5cm). Put the pot in a greenhouse, propagator or on a bright windowsill.

◆ **WHEN THE ROOTS** begin to show through the bottom of the pots, transfer the seedlings into 5in (12cm) pots.

pumpkin

Hardening off Before planting out, the seedlings should be hardened off in a cold frame for a few days.

Planting out

Choose a sunny, sheltered spot and dig in plenty of well-rotted manure or compost to improve the soil before planting your seedlings. Position each on a slightly raised mound of earth at a spacing of 3–6ft (1–2m) to give them room to ramble. Firm the seedlings in and water thoroughly. Mulch around each plant after watering.

Dig a hole Create a hole large enough for the root ball, then slide the seedling out of its pot.

Firm in Firm the seedling in and mulch around it with well-rotted manure.

Regular feeding Pumpkins need fertilizing regularly; if their leaves start to turn yellow, it's a sign that they need feeding.

Routine care

◆ **FEED PLANTS** weekly with a general-purpose liquid fertilizer or tomato fertilizer. The potassium will develop their color, size, and flavor.

◆ **PLACE A** thick layer of mulch around each plant to conserve moisture and suppress weeds.

◆ **REMOVE SOME** of the fruitlets before they get too big, leaving just two or three on the plant so that it puts its energy into producing larger fruit.

◆ **KEEP THE AREA** around young plants well weeded so they don't have to compete for nutrients and water.

◆ **THE FRUIT** is ready to harvest from late September to early November. When the stems crack and the skin hardens, it means that the fruit is ready. If possible, leave the pumpkins to dry in the fall sun for a week or two, then, before the first frost, cut them off, leaving a length of stalk attached to prevent rotting.

Large specimens

If you want really big fruit, choose large varieties. Remove most of the fruitlets, leaving just two or three on each plant. Feed weekly and you should get large-sized pumpkins.

Stop the rot Place large pumpkins on bricks, tiles, or blocks of wood to prevent them from rotting into the soil.

Storing & Using

They can be used in: soups...curries...casseroles...pies...ravioli...risottos...bread...or roasted...or frozen...

Pumpkins store extremely well if they are properly "cured," which means letting their skins harden fully in the sun for 10 days or so after harvesting. Store them for up to 6 months in a cool, dry place. You can also purée the peeled pumpkin, divide it into portions, and freeze for up to 6 months.

Pumpkin butter This delicious sweet spread is made by cooking pumpkin with apple juice and spices. It will keep for up to 6 months in the refrigerator.

Pumpkin pie Traditionally eaten at Thanksgiving, this dessert is made using pumpkin, eggs, milk, sugar, and spices, and served with whipped cream.

Pumpkin seeds Roast these in the oven on a baking tray, drizzled with a little olive oil and sprinkled with red pepper flakes. The result will be a healthy, tasty snack.

Halloween

The most recognizable symbol of Halloween is a pumpkin carved into a Jack-o'-lantern. Children love them, and what could be more fun than to carve your own homegrown pumpkin? Search the internet for unusual ideas for carving elaborate designs, but if that's not for you, just use a sharp knife to carve a smiley—or scary if you prefer—face. Pop a tealight inside for the full effect.

Waste not Don't waste the flesh of your pumpkin. You can use it to make soup or pumpkin pie.

Squash

Squash is divided up into two categories: winter and summer types. Summer squash come in a wide range of sizes and colors, and are very closely related to zucchini. Winter squash are tougher, heartier vegetables, more like pumpkins, but with a nuttier, sweeter taste and a wide range of quirky and unusual shapes. Both types are easy to grow.

Planting out Seedlings can be planted out once the risk of frost is over but will need watering daily until they get established.

Storing & Using

They can be used in: soups ...stews...stir-fries...or roasted...or baked...

Winter squash can be stored for up to 6 months in a cool, dry place. "Cure" them first by hardening the skin in a sunny spot, but keep them dry. The skin of summer squash doesn't harden as much as winter squash, so these can't be kept as long.

Roasted Peeled, sliced, drizzled with olive oil and sprinkled with fresh, aromatic herbs, squash can be oven-roasted to make a tasty side dish.

Growing

If you want a bumper crop from your squash, you must give them a rich, fertile soil in full sun. If you are restricted for space, try growing some of the smaller-fruiting varieties up vertical supports such as pergolas, trellises, and posts.

◆ **SOW SEEDS** under cover from mid- to late spring, individually in 3in (7.5cm) pots and ½in (1cm) deep. Sow them on their sides to prevent them from rotting. Leave them to germinate on a sunny window ledge, then plant them out 5ft (1.5m) apart when there is no further risk of spring frost.

◆ **ALTERNATIVELY**, sow directly outdoors after the risk of frost is over, sowing two or three seeds 1in (2.5cm) deep and 5ft (1.5m) apart. Thin the seedlings out to leave the strongest and cover with row cover or a cloche if a late frost is forecast.

'Queensland Blue'   'Sweet Dumpling'   butternut

Squash bed

If you have poor, infertile soil in your garden, do not worry. You can easily and cheaply construct a squash bed, where you can provide the perfect growing conditions for your beautiful crop. The bed can be as big as you have room for. The cardboard base retains moisture and nutrients, and eventually rots away. Feed the squash regularly to ensure a large crop.

Cardboard base Lay pieces of cardboard on the bare soil and create a retaining wall all around from brick and rocks or wood.

Organic matter Add plenty of organic matter to the bed, such as well-rotted manure or good garden compost.

Plant and water Space the plants at least 4ft (1.2m) apart and water them every few days throughout the summer.

Routine care

Because they produce so much luxuriant foliage and their fruit has such a high water content, squash are really thirsty plants, so make sure you visit them regularly throughout the summer to give them plenty of water.

◆ **SUPPORT SQUASH** on a piece of wood, tile, or straw to stop them from rotting on the ground as they start to swell. Regularly tie in the growth if you are training them up posts and stakes.

◆ **TOUGHEN UP** squash for storing over winter, by leaving the fruit to mature on the plant for as long as possible before the first frost arrives. Don't leave the fruit out in the frost, or it will turn mushy and won't keep for long.

Netting Some squash have a trailing habit and, if space is limited, can be trained vertically. As the fruit start to swell, they will need support. Here, a fruit net from store-bought produce does the job.

'Turk's Turban'

'Little Gem'

pattypan

Bell peppers & Chiles

Coming in a range of vibrant colors, bell peppers and chiles spice up your garden with eye-catching fruit, as well as enhance your cooking. Bell peppers put the crunch into salads while chiles vary from mild to fiery hot. Match your culinary preference to your plant choice.

Water Keep plants well watered throughout the summer to produce a good crop. Dry spells can result in fewer fruit on the plants.

Sowing

Sow seeds indoors in early spring, placing the pots in a heated propagator until the seedlings have sprouted.

Pots Place seeds ½in (1cm) deep in seed-starting mix in individual pots and water well. Once the seedlings have emerged, move to a warm window ledge.

Planting out When all danger of frost has passed, space plants at 16in (40cm) apart in the soil. Water thoroughly after planting.

Growing

Bell peppers and chiles are suitable for growing outdoors in the garden if there is a warm, sunny site available. Alternatively, they can be grown in the greenhouse but this means having to get out to the garden each day to water the plants. If the garden is in a frost pocket, then you should definitely grow them under cover.

◆ **CHILES AND BELL PEPPERS** can either be grown in the ground or in cold-resistant containers that are at least 10in (25cm) wide. Plants can also be planted into growing bags, but these will need watering every day.

◆ **IF PLANTING OUTDOORS,** the seedlings should be hardened off for a few days beforehand, either by putting them in a cold frame or by placing them outdoors during the day and bringing them back inside at night.

◆ **PINCH BACK** the growing tips when the plants are about 10in (25cm) tall to encourage the plants to grow bushier. This should help the plant produce more fruit. Once you see flowers on the plants, start giving them weekly liquid fertilizer to help them develop and then produce fruit.

habanero   'Cascabel'   'Aji Limon'   'Aji'   'Ring O Fire'

purple bell pepper

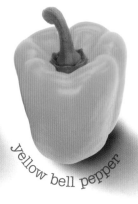

red bell pepper

yellow bell pepper

Support

As they grow, the plants will need supporting with stakes and soft garden twine to keep the stems from snapping.

Root care When inserting the stake into the soil, take care not to damage the roots of the plants.

Routine care

If you are growing plants in the greenhouse, flying insects won't be able to reach the flowers to pollinate them so they will need assistance. Stroke the insides of the flowers with a small paintbrush to pass the pollen from one flower to another.

◆ **HARVEST** the fruit when it is green or when it has fully colored up. Use pruners to remove them from the plant.

◆ **PLACE A CLOCHE** over the bell pepper plants to protect them if they haven't ripened before fall.

Storing & Using

They can be used for: chili...salsa...or dried... or roasted...or frozen...or canned...

Bell peppers become mushy when frozen, but can be used in soups and stews. Chiles are best stored dried, but can also be frozen and will keep for up to a year in the freezer. Dry in the sun on wire mesh, or hang up in the kitchen. Always wash your hands after handling chiles.

Chile oil Chiles can be used to infuse cooking oil or can be diced and added to relishes.

Drying Thread chiles onto lengths of raffia then hang them up to dry in the kitchen.

pimento

'Hungarian Hot Wax'

'Poblano'

Scotch bonnet

cayenne

Sweet corn

Tall, leafy, and upright, sweet corn is one of the most attractive crops to grow in the garden. It is also one of the most worthwhile, since the ears taste the sweetest right after they are picked, which you will only appreciate fully when you cook your own, straight from the plants. The ears can be boiled, microwaved, or cooked directly on the grill.

Ready When the tassels of the sweet corn begin to turn brown, check if the ears are ready to eat (see right).

Growing tubes If you sow the seeds in cardboard tubes, you can plant out the entire tube to avoid disturbing the roots of the plants.

Growing

To give your crop a head start, sow seed under cover in late spring. Fill small pots or cell flats with seed-starting mix, water lightly, then sow one seed in each pot or cell. Seed can also be sown directly outside (see below).

◆ **THE SEED** should be planted ¾in (2cm) deep and then covered over with soil mix. Place in a heated propagator or on a warm sunny windowsill.

◆ **SEEDLINGS CAN** be planted out after the risk of spring frost has passed. The plants should be about 4in (10cm) tall before planting out.

◆ **SWEET CORN** relies on being pollinated by the wind, which is most successful if the seedlings are planted in a grid pattern, where the pollen can blow from plant to plant. Position plants 12 x 12in (30 x 30cm) apart.

Sowing outdoors

It is possible to sow seeds directly into the soil from mid-spring onward, which is useful if you don't have a greenhouse. Warm the soil using row cover for about two weeks before sowing. Make small planting holes, ¾in (2cm) deep, spaced 12in (30cm) apart in a grid pattern, and sow two seeds in each. Cover the seeds with soil. Replace the cover until the seeds germinate, then thin the seedlings to leave the strongest one.

Sowing Sow two seeds in each hole to double your chances of successful germination. Not all seeds will come up or survive.

Germination When the seedlings start to emerge, they should be thinned out, leaving the strongest plant.

Protecting plants Recycle your plastic bottles or milk cartons to use as extra weather protection for the plants.

Growing tips

Sweet corn varieties should not be allowed to cross-pollinate each other because this can spoil the corn. Either grow one variety or plant different varieties well apart from each other. As the plants get taller, they will need staking to provide support. To make the best use of the space, grow low-growing squash, which will trail across the soil, beneath sweet corn plants.

Weeding Weed regularly around the base of the plants to prevent any weeds from competing for nutrients.

Mounding As the plants develop, mound the soil up around their bases to provide additional support to the tall stems.

Watering Plants will need watering every few days, particularly after planting and at flowering time.

Harvesting

Sweet corn is harvested by firmly twisting the ears from the plant. You can expect two or three ears from a healthy plant.

◆ **TO TEST** if they're ready, peel back the outer leaves and press your thumbnail into a kernel. If a milky sap runs out of it, they're ready for harvesting. If not, wrap the leaves back around the cob and check it a few days later.

When to harvest
Sweet corn ears soon lose their sweetness once ripe. Check them regularly and harvest them as soon as possible.

Storing & Using

It can be used for: soups...cornbread...relish...or can be roasted...or frozen...

Ideally, eat the sweet corn as soon as possible after harvesting to enjoy the natural sweetness and flavor to its full. Harvested cobs can be kept refrigerated for no longer than a day or two at the most. Frozen ears keep well for around 6 months.

Freezing Like peas, corn can often taste sweeter after freezing. Freeze ears whole or, if space is limited, remove kernels and then freeze.

Relish Sweet corn kernels can be added to relishes, salsas, and chutneys, providing natural sweetness and color.

Cornbread Savory cornbread is a tasty and traditional dish. It can be flavored using chiles, cheese, or herbs.

sweet corn

Globe artichokes

Adding a wonderful ornamental element to the kitchen garden with their architectural, silvery foliage and stunning bright purple flower heads, globe artichokes are also a gourmet feast. They are large plants but don't expect heavy crops—the edible flower hearts are a harvest of quality not quantity.

Seeds and offsets

Artichokes can be grown from seed in mid-spring but should not be allowed to crop in their first year and will yield only sparingly their second. Mature plants crop more freely.

Sowing Lightly water the potting mix before sowing the seeds thinly in flats at a depth of ¾in (2cm). Grow the plants until large enough to plant outside.

New plants Artichokes can be grown from leafy buds, or offsets, that form at the base of the parent plant. Cut them off in spring, pot up, and grow them on.

Growing

These are a real luxury crop to grow since they take up a lot of space in relation to their yield. However, they are well worth the effort because they taste amazing and are expensive to buy. The plants require a sheltered location in full sun, in rich but well-drained soil.

◆ **DUE TO** their elegant and stately habit, you might want to consider planting artichokes in the flower border, rather than the vegetable garden.

◆ **BEAR IN MIND** when deciding where to grow artichokes that they are large perennial plants and require plenty of space over a prolonged period. They are, therefore, not ideal for smaller plots.

Hardening off Harden off seedlings for a few days on a porch or in a cold frame before planting out.

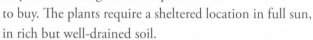

'Green Globe Improved'

'Purple Artichoke'

Flowers Gardeners have to choose whether they want to harvest the artichokes or allow the striking purple, thistlelike flowers to develop each year.

Overwintering

Artichokes are perennial and are at their most productive for about three or four years after planting. When the plants start to die back in fall, the dead material should be removed to prevent any buildup of disease.

Cutting back After harvesting, the plants should be cut back and a thick layer of mulch added to suppress weeds and protect the central growing point.

Routine care

Seedlings and offsets should be planted out in late spring, spacing the plants 3ft (90cm) apart. Remove any flower buds that appear in the first year to encourage strong growth.

◆ **KEEP THE SOIL** around the plants well mulched with garden compost and water regularly during dry periods, particularly while the plants are young.

◆ **HARVEST BY** removing the artichoke head using pruners when it is about the size of a golf ball. If left too long, the flower will start to open, and the hearts will become inedible.

Ready to eat Cut the artichoke buds when they reach full size but before the outer scales have begun to open.

Storing & Using

They can be: steamed...boiled... grilled...added to salads...or dips...or risottos...

Cut and cook artichokes right away, or store in the refrigerator for a day or two at the most. Don't freeze them. They are delicious with garlic mayonnaise, or lemon and olive oil dressing.

Division Plants can be divided after three or four years—use two forks back-to-back to do this. Offshoots can be potted as replacement plants.

vegetables
beans & pods

green & string beans
• a string bean support •
fava beans
• peas & snow peas

Green & String beans

Brightly colored flowers scrambling up a rustic tepee structure is a classic image in a kitchen garden. String beans are more rampant than green beans, but both require structures to climb up, providing not only a splash of color in the garden plot, but also height to what could otherwise be a flat-looking vegetable patch.

'Purple Teepee'

Sowing

Both types of beans can be sown indoors or outside in late spring. Sowing under cover gets them off to a faster start, but outdoors is fine and means you don't have to harden them off before planting out.

Indoors Fill small plastic pots or toilet paper rolls with multi-purpose potting mix. Make a 2in (5cm) deep hole, sow the seed, and fill the hole.

Outdoors Make a 2in (5cm) deep hole directly into the soil. Place two seeds in each hole. After the seeds have germinated, remove the weaker plant of the two.

Growing

If you have sown your seeds indoors, they will need planting out in early summer, once the risk of frost has passed. Choose a sheltered location in full sun. Thoroughly dig over the area to be planted, remove any weeds from the site, and add plenty of organic material, such as well-rotted manure or garden compost.

◆ **WATER REGULARLY** throughout the summer, especially once the plants start to flower and produce pods. Dry spells can cause the flowers to die back, and developing pods may wither.

◆ **THE BEANS** are ready for harvesting when they reach about 6in (15cm) long. Pick string beans before the pods start to swell or they will lose their tenderness and become tough and stringy.

◆ **KEEP PICKING** regularly, almost every day, to keep the plants in full production. Otherwise, they will quickly turn to seed and stop cropping. Green beans can be harvested for their pods or as mature beans, depending on the variety.

green beans

Support structure Bamboo stakes and tall sticks both make very good supports for beans. Position one plant at the base of each support.

Support

Climbing beans require supports, which are commonly made from tall sticks or bamboo stakes, at least 7–8ft (2.1–2.4m) tall. These can be arranged as circular tepees, or as double rows joined across the top to form a long, rigid structure. The uprights should be placed 8–9in (20–23cm) apart.

◆ **AS PLANTS GROW** they may need tying to their supports at first. After this they will naturally climb up the structures using their twining stems to grip the uprights. Particularly vigorous plants may occasionally need tying in throughout the season. Pinch back the growing tips when they reach the top to encourage plants to produce new stems and more beans.

◆ **IT IS BEST** to have the supports in place first before planting, to avoid damaging the plants later.

Growing tips

Both types of beans are relatively trouble-free. String bean leaves can be prone to wind damage, leaving them tattered. Keep damaged plants well watered to aid recovery.

Protection Upside-down plastic bottles protect young plants from slug attack and from late-spring frost.

Tying in Occasional wayward shoots may need tying in to the climbing structure as the beans grow.

Mulching Beans will benefit from a layer of mulch around their roots to help retain soil moisture.

Storing & Using

They can be used for: relish...chutney...casseroles... salads...or can be frozen...

Green and string beans are best eaten fresh, but can be stored in the refrigerator for a few days. Green beans can be left to develop fully in their pods, which, when dried, can be used as navy beans. Store them in an airtight container for up to a year and use them in casseroles and bean salads. Both string and green beans can be frozen; blanch first, then dry and freeze. They will keep well in the freezer for 9 months.

Chutney String beans often produce a big crop. There are plenty of exciting bean chutney recipes that will allow you to enjoy your harvest all year.

string beans

Project
String bean support

String beans are very easy to grow and can be started off in pots under cover in early May. By June they will be ready to plant out but, being climbing plants, they will need a good support system. This project features the traditional and very common double-row method that makes taking care of your crop and harvesting far easier.

The stakes should be inserted at an angle sloping toward the middle of the plot so that each pair of stakes almost touches at the top.

Alternative shapes

Being such active climbers, string beans will happily find their way up any nearby structure. If you don't have room for the traditional double row of stakes shown here, then trellis or garden fencing with vertical wires attached to it will work just as well. You could also make an attractive arch using flexible stakes.

The soil should be prepared before planting. Dig it over thoroughly and add plenty of organic material. Well-rotted compost or leaf mold are ideal choices. These will help the soil to retain moisture.

Popular pyramids A pyramid is a popular shape for supporting string beans. Insert four stakes in the ground at the corners of an imaginary square and tie the tops of the four stakes together.

MATERIALS & TOOLS

- bamboo or garden stakes, 8ft (2.4m) long (the quantity required will depend on the length of your plot), garden twine

1 Push in the first of your stakes at one corner of the plot. Using another stake as a guide for a straight line, continue pushing the stakes in at intervals of 6–12in (15–30cm).

2 Once the row is complete, repeat the procedure with the other set of stakes, positioning them 18–24in (45–60cm) away and parallel to the first row.

The top and final stake anchors the pairs of stakes securely and helps to keep them properly spaced as the string beans grow.

step 3

step 4

step 5

Tie the twine around the stakes tightly so that the completed structure is rigid and there is no risk of it collapsing.

Plants can be encouraged to grow upward by gently wrapping their stems around the stakes. You can use a little loosely wound twine to hold the stems in place until they start to grow.

3   With all the stakes in place, lay another stake horizontally across the top so that it sits in the natural cradle created by the other stakes.

4   Securely tie the horizontal stake to each pair of stakes, starting at one end and working your way across to the other end.

5   Plant a string-bean plant in a prepared hole at the base of each stake. Fill the hole with soil, then gently firm it in place.

Ensure you have easy access to both sides of your string bean supports so you can easily pinch back the tips of plants that have reached the top, and to make it easy to harvest your crop.

Fava beans

Fava beans are one of the first vegetables to harvest from the garden, and many gardeners compete to see who will be the first to pick their fresh crop of these small and succulent vegetables each spring. Their sweetly scented white flowers are also fantastic for attracting bees and many other pollinating insects.

Sowing outdoors In dry weather, water the furrow first, then sow the seeds, cover over, and firm the soil.

Sowing outdoors

In milder areas it is possible to sow fava beans directly outdoors in the fall for an early crop the following spring. To do this it is necessary to use hardy varieties such as 'Express' and 'Statissa'. Otherwise they should be sown outdoors in early or mid-spring.

◆ **PRIOR TO** sowing, prepare the soil well by digging it over and raking it level. Fava beans are more tolerant of poor soils than other beans.

◆ **SOW BEANS** 2in (5cm) deep and 8in (20cm) apart, although there are dwarf varieties that can be sown at closer distances.

Watering Keep young plants well watered; they will soon develop a deep taproot to reach groundwater supplies.

Sowing under cover

If you are on an exposed site or in a cold region, making fall outdoor sowing unrealistic, then seeds can be sown under cover in mid- to late winter. Seeds should be sown 2in (5cm) deep in potting mix and watered during germination.

Pots Use growing tubes or toilet paper rolls to help the long taproots get established.

Harden off Harden off the plants in a cold frame or at home on the porch before planting out.

Plant out Plant them 8in (20cm) apart and be ready to cover with row cover in cold weather.

Routine care

Plants that have been started indoors may get frost damaged, so be ready with some row cover if cold weather is forecast. Taller varieties will need support, so push twigs in among emerging plants. Give the soil a thorough soaking during dry periods in the spring, particularly during flowering. Make successional sowings (that is, sow a new batch every three weeks or so) through early and mid-spring to extend the growing season into summer.

◆ **BEANS SHOULD** be ready about ten weeks after sowing in spring. Pick the pods when they are young, starting at the base of the plant and working upward as the season progresses.

◆ **WHEN THE PLANTS** have finished producing pods, cut them down to ground level. This allows the roots to break down in the soil and provides a free supply of nitrogen for the next crop.

Growing tips

Pinching back the growing tip encourages an even earlier spring crop. Pinching back the tip also reduces damage by the black bean aphid, which attacks the young shoots.

Pinching back Pinch back the growing tip by about 3in (7.5cm) when the first pods start to form along the stem. The tips can be eaten.

Companion planting Growing a native plant near fava beans attracts hoverflies, which feed on blackflies.

Storing & Using

They can be used for: risotto...soups...stews...dips...or frozen...

Fava beans are incredibly versatile and deliciously tender when young and fresh. They can be kept in the refrigerator for a few days or can be frozen for up to 6 months. Use older beans for soups and stews. Cook fresh young beans until al dente, combine with a little garlic, butter, and herbs for a side dish with meat or fish.

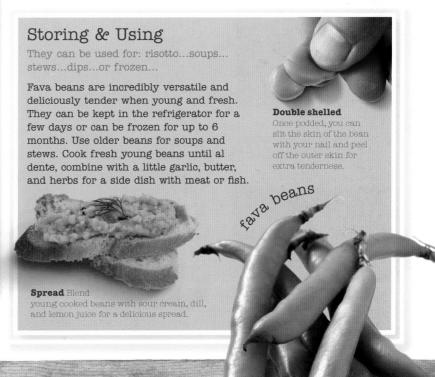

Double shelled Once podded, you can slit the skin of the bean with your nail and peel off the outer skin for extra tenderness.

Spread Blend young cooked beans with sour cream, dill, and lemon juice for a delicious spread.

fava beans

Peas & Snow peas

These climbing and scrambling plants are a garden must; there is nothing quite like their sweet taste and crunchy texture when picked fresh, and they can be expensive to buy at the store. If space is a problem, then consider growing some of the dwarf varieties.

Healthy snack Snow peas are real kid pleasers and must be one of the most healthy packed-lunch snacks available. Keep picking to ensure they keep producing delicious pods.

Sowing indoors

Sow peas and snow peas indoors in February or March, or outside in spring. Alternatively, sow them indoors in fall for an early crop the following season.

Sow in pots Place a couple of seeds into small plastic pots filled with good-quality potting mix. Seeds should be about 2in (5cm) deep.

Thin out Keep the plants warm and well watered. Thin out the weaker shoots and plant the stronger ones out in spring when all danger of frost is over.

Growing

Peas and snow peas require a location in full sun that is sheltered from strong winds to prevent pollinating insects from being blown away when they visit the blooms. Peas require plenty of moisture in the soil so they can produce masses of flowers and pods during the summer.

◆ **TO HOLD MOISTURE** in the soil, dig out a trench 12in (30cm) deep in fall and fill it with well-rotted compost, kitchen waste, and shredded newspaper.

◆ **COVER IT** over with a 2in (5cm) layer of soil and leave it to rot down for a few weeks prior to sowing or planting.

Sowing outside

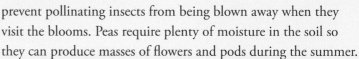

Peas either have smooth or wrinkly skins. The smooth-skinned ones are hardier and more suitable for early sowings, while the wrinkly-skinned types produce sweeter crops. Sow every three or four weeks until midsummer for a long season.

Sowing Sow seeds in trenches 2in (5cm) deep, 5in (12cm) wide, and 3in (8cm) apart.

Thin out Keep seedlings well watered and thin out any that are growing too close together.

Routine care

Apart from providing support (see right) and plenty of water (see below), you don't need to give peas and snow peas many special amenities.

◆ **PLANTS NEED** to be kept well watered, particularly during the flowering period and when they are producing their pods. Healthy, well-watered plants are also less prone to mildew.

◆ **WATCH OUT FOR BIRDS**, particularly pigeons, which love stripping off the pea shoots. Covering the plants with a net will help to protect them.

◆ **KEEP PICKING** peas and snow peas as they mature and sow regularly to be able to harvest throughout the summer.

Support

Unless you are growing dwarf varieties, peas and snow peas need a support to scramble up. Choose from pea sticks, netting, or chicken wire.

Sticks Peas sticks are the most effective method of support. Insert small branches next to the plants when they are 3in (7.5cm) high.

Storing & Using

They can be used for: soups...stir-fries...salads...or can be frozen...

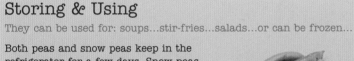

Both peas and snow peas keep in the refrigerator for a few days. Snow peas are flat-podded peas eaten whole. Crisp and sweet, they can be eaten raw in salads, steamed, or used in stir-fries. Peas are good eaten fresh, raw or cooked, or added to side dishes.

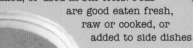

Soup Fresh peas make a delicious soup with some mint and a swirl of cream or some sour cream.

Frozen Peas are one of the few vegetables that almost benefit from freezing. Picked and frozen immediately, they retain their sweetness and can be kept in the freezer for up to 9 months.

Training Keep a watch out for any wayward stems and hook them back onto the twigs if any are growing away from their support.

peas in their pods

snow peas

vegetables
bulbs & roots

potatoes • carrots • sweet potatoes • onions & shallots • garlic • green onions • drying rack • Florence fennel & kohlrabi • celery root & parsnips • rutabagas & turnips • beets • radishes • Jerusalem artichokes

Potatoes

There are three types of potatoes, descriptively named, called early, main, and storage. It is definitely worth growing these in the garden, but if you are short of space, avoid main varieties, which are bulky. Instead, focus on growing new potatoes and salad types, which also have the best flavor.

Chitting

Get your potatoes off to an early start by getting them to sprout, or "chit," before planting. This method is particularly useful on cold, wet soil for early or new potatoes.

Early start Place seed potatoes with their rose ends (where the buds are) facing upward in egg cartons in a light, cool, frost-free place until they sprout.

Growing

Plant early and main potatoes in early spring; main can be planted in mid-spring. To plant, dig a trench 8in (20cm) deep and place the seed potatoes along the bottom at spacings of 18in (45cm) for early potatoes, 28in (70cm) for main.

◆ **MAKE SURE** the potatoes are the right way up with their eyes, or "chits," facing upward. Mix well-rotted manure or compost with the soil from the trench, and use this to cover over the potatoes.

◆ **POTATOES** require a sunny site, ideally with heavy, rich soil. If you have an overgrown garden, planting potatoes will help to break up the soil.

◆ **ONLY PLANT** seed potatoes that are certified virus-free, and don't raise plants from tubers left in the soil from last year, which can harbor disease.

Planting in bags If you are short of space, grow potatoes in large bags or special potato bags. Tip the plants out to harvest the tubers or carefully dig them up.

Planting When the sprouts are about 1in (2.5cm) long, the potatoes are ready to be planted out into holes or trenches.

'All Blue' 'Atlantic' 'Kennebec' 'International Kidney'

Protection Early-emerging shoots can be susceptible to cold damage, so make sure they are covered with row cover.

Hilling up

As the shoots emerge they need hilling up—covering the base of plants with soil. This helps to prevent cold damage, stops the growing tubers from turning green, and encourages a larger crop.

Cover up To hill up potatoes, use a spade or rake to push soil up around the base of the shoots, ensuring the soil doesn't cover the foliage.

Routine care

Once planted, potatoes need little routine care and are among the easiest crops to grow. Young plants should be weeded regularly to prevent competition for moisture and nutrients. Mature plants form canopies of leaves that suppress most weeds.

◆ **KEEP THE PLANTS** well watered as they grow, especially during dry spells. If kept too dry, the plants will produce smaller tubers and poorer harvests.

◆ **FEED THE PLANTS** regularly using a balanced, granular fertilizer.

◆ **CHECK THE TUBERS** by scraping back the soil carefully to see if they are ready to harvest—re-cover if not.

◆ **FOR AN EARLY START**, try growing potatoes in wooden crates, which will insulate them from frost in the spring.

Harvest Potatoes are ready for harvesting just after flowering. Use a garden fork to dig up the potatoes, being careful not to damage the tubers.

Storing & Using

They can be: mashed...boiled...fried...roasted... baked...or prepared as chips...or au gratin...

Potatoes are probably the most popular and versatile of vegetables. New potatoes, such as 'Norkoth' or 'Yukon Gold', are great in salads. Use main types, such as 'Red Thumb', for mashed potatoes, 'King Edward' for baking, and 'All Blue' for roasting.

Storing Thick paper sacks are ideal for storage. Kept in a cool, dark place, the potatoes will store well for 2–3 months or more.

'King Edward'   'Norkoth'   'Yukon Gold'   'Vivaldi'   'Red Thumb'

Carrots

These delicious, sweet, and crunchy roots are a real favorite of children, and if stored correctly, they can be enjoyed all year round. Consider growing them in raised beds if you have rocky or heavy soil. For something different, consider growing the purple varieties, the original color of carrots prior to the 17th century.

Sowing

Avoid using old seeds and check the expiration date on the packet—this can often cause poor or no germination. Carrots should be directly sown into the soil in spring.

Starting off Make a furrow, ¾in (2cm) deep, and sow seeds lightly. Use row cover early in the year to protect against cold.

Thinning out When they emerge, thin out the seedlings. Check the seed packet for their space requirements.

Growing carrots

There are a wide range of carrot varieties to grow, but they all generally prefer light, well-drained soil in full sun. If the soil in the garden is heavy or rocky, then consider growing them in raised beds. Alternatively, try growing the short or round varieties such as 'Parmex', which cope better in these conditions.

◆ **DIG OVER** the beds thoroughly before sowing, removing any large rocks and weeds. Improve the soil with well-rotted organic matter. Avoid using fresh manure, which can cause roots to split.

◆ **IN SPRING** sow seeds in batches, every 2–3 weeks, to give a prolonged harvest. The seeds can be slow to germinate so don't give up too soon.

Watering Keep young seedlings well watered in dry spells to assist the plants to develop and their roots to swell.

heritage carrots

Carrot rust flies This pest can quickly destroy a crop. Prevent damage by erecting a 24in (60cm) barrier of insect mesh around the crop to keep the low-flying adults from landing.

short, round carrots

long, stump-rooted carrots

Routine care

If growing carrots early in the year, they will need covering with row cover to speed up germination and protect the seedlings. Lift the cover on warmer days to maximize the light reaching the plants.

Keep the plants well watered in dry spells and regularly weed around them, being careful not to damage their roots.

- ◆ **CARROT RUST FLIES** (see p.232) are the main pest to watch for; their larvae will tunnel into the roots and ruin the crop. Thinning, harvesting, and even weeding can release the scent of the carrots, attracting the pest, so do these jobs in the evening when the insects are inactive.
- ◆ **IF THERE IS** a major problem with carrot rust flies, use resistant varieties such as 'Flyaway'.

Harvesting Lift carrots once they reach the desired size. Early varieties should be pulled when young, tender, and juicy.

(see p.232)

Storing & Using

They can be used for: soups...stews...stir-fries... or boiled...or roasted...

Carrots will keep for a few days in the refrigerator, or blanch and store in the freezer for up to 9 months.

In sand Carrots last for weeks stored in boxes of slightly damp sand, kept in a cool, dark place.

long, pointed carrots

Sweet potatoes

Sweet potatoes are a wonderful alternative to the humble spud. Traditionally considered an exotic crop from warm climates, recently developed varieties enable gardeners living in cooler parts of the world to enjoy this delicious vegetable, too. Low in fat and packed full of vitamins and antioxidants, sweet potatoes are definitely worth giving a try.

Watering This crop needs regular watering—daily in dry weather. To avoid watering as frequently, cut plastic bottles in half, push them into the soil alongside the plants and fill with water.

Growing

Sweet potatoes require a temperature of at least 70°F (21°C) to produce their tasty underground tubers. In cooler climates you will need to grow them in a polytunnel, cloche, or greenhouse. In warmer areas they can be grown outdoors but will benefit from being planted in a hole cut through black weed-barrier fabric to help maintain the temperature of the soil.

◆ **MAIL-ORDER PLANTS** arrive in spring as slips, or rooted cuttings. As soon as they arrive, plunge the slips into a bucket of water indoors to revitalize them, then pot them into individual pots in general-purpose potting mix the following day. Keep the slips indoors for three weeks before planting them out.

◆ **SWEET POTATOES** are space hungry, eventually becoming large, vigorous, sprawling plants, so make sure you have enough room for them. They should be planted 12in (30cm) apart in rows 30in (75cm) apart.

◆ **THEY REQUIRE** a sheltered, fertile, warm site in well-drained soil. Dig the soil over thoroughly prior to planting and add plenty of well-rotted organic matter.

Pruning

Sweet potatoes are vigorous, sprawling plants whose growth must be kept in check if they are to focus their energy on producing a crop—and to prevent them from smothering other plants. If you are growing them in a greenhouse, you can train the stems onto a support system to keep them out of the way. When cutting back new growth (see right), save the leaves and cook as you would spinach.

Encouraging laterals Regularly prune back the new growth to encourage more laterals to develop on the plant.

sweet potato

Storing & Using

They can be used in: soups...curries...as fries...
or mashed...or roasted...or sautéed...or frozen...

Sweet potatoes are neither very sweet nor very moist
when they are first harvested, so keep them in a
warm place for a week to cure them before eating.
If preferred, after curing, move them to a cool, dark
place and you can keep them for about a month. If
you want to freeze them, cook them
first. They will keep for up to 12
months in the freezer.

Frittata Teamed with eggs, green onions
and cayenne pepper, this frittata makes
a tasty light lunch or elegant supper
dish served with a fresh green salad.

Bake Sweet
potatoes can
be oven-baked
like an ordinary
potato and filled
with a range
of toppings.

Sweet fries Tossed in oil and
soy sauce or red pepper flakes,
these sweet potato fries make a
good accompaniment to homemade
burgers or chicken dishes
and contain more fiber
than traditional potatoes.
Serve with sour cream.

Routine care

Feed the sweet potato plants with a good, general-
purpose fertilizer every few weeks.

◆ **WATER EVERY FEW DAYS** in dry weather (see
opposite) and particularly if you are growing them
under cover. Keep the greenhouse, polytunnel, or
cloche well ventilated on warm days.

◆ **THE FOLIAGE** turning brown and starting to die,
about three months after planting, is a sign that they
are ready to harvest. Dig them up, making sure that
you don't spike them with the fork, or leave them in
the ground for longer if preferred, but make sure to
lift them before the first fall frost.

Harvesting Sweet
potato tubers grow
underground like
common or garden
potatoes and are
harvested in the
same way. They
come in a huge
range of colors,
including orange
and purple, which
add a splash of
color to the plate.

'Boniato'

Onions & Shallots

The humble onion has to be the number one essential vegetable to grow in the garden if you enjoy cooking, because they appear in most culinary dishes. Shallots are a smaller, more delicately flavored version but they still pack a punch in terms of taste and versatility in the kitchen.

Sowing indoors

Onion seeds can be sown under cover from midwinter to mid-spring. Sowing onions from seed takes longer than planting sets, but is cheaper to do, and there is a wider range of varieties to try.

Sowing seeds Fill cell packs or small plastic pots with good-quality seed-starting mix and sow clusters of seeds in each one, ½in (1cm) deep.

Thinning seedlings When the seedlings are about 3in (7.5cm) tall, they should be thinned out to leave the strongest one in each pot or cell.

Growing

Onions and shallots are one of the easiest and least demanding crops to grow. Onion seeds can either be sown indoors (see left) or directly in the soil. However, they are more commonly grown from sets (see below). The plants require a sheltered location in well-drained soil in full sun. They prefer light soils, since they can be prone to rotting in heavy, wet conditions.

◆ **TRY GROWING** them in raised beds if the soil is unsuitable.

◆ **SHALLOTS GROW** very slowly from seed, so it is recommended that they are planted as sets in early spring or fall, at 6in (15cm) intervals, in rows 12in (30cm) apart.

Grow bunches Instead of thinning the seedlings, onions and shallots can be left to grow in bunches, giving a large number of smaller bulbs.

Planting sets

The easiest method of growing onions is to plant sets. These are baby bulbs that grow and mature once planted. Planting time is usually spring, although overwintering types and Japanese onions can also be planted in the fall.

Spacing Onions sets should be spaced at 2–4in (5–10cm) intervals, in rows that are 12in (30cm) apart.

Firming in Push the sets firmly into the soil, leaving just the tips poking out above the surface.

white onion

red onion

yellow onion

Harvesting

Onions and shallots are ready to lift when the foliage yellows and dies back. Bend the leaves over as the bulbs mature.

Onions Mature bulbs should have dry, crisp outer skins before they are harvested and stored. Leave them to dry.

Shallots Mature shallots form clusters of small bulbs, which are split and used individually in the kitchen.

Routine care

Onions and shallots are relatively trouble-free. Keep them well watered during dry periods but be careful not to overwater them —onions will start to rot if they set in wet soil for too long. Stop watering completely as the bulbs start to mature, since the excess moisture will prevent the bulbs from drying after harvesting.

◆ **CAREFULLY WEED** between plants to prevent competition for nutrients. A short-handled onion hoe is useful to reach weeds in the gaps without damaging the bulbs.

◆ **ONIONS THAT** were planted or sown in fall should be ready for harvesting in midsummer, while spring-raised plants will be ready in summer and fall.

◆ **ONIONS AND SHALLOTS** should be dried in the sun before taking them inside for storage. If the weather is dry, leave them on the soil surface for a day or two.

Storing & Using

They can be used in: sauces...stews...casseroles...salsa... French onion soup... or can be pickled...or strung...

Onions and shallots store very well if dried properly and can keep for up to a year hanging up in the kitchen. Red onions are good for slicing into salads, while yellow ones are stronger and are better cooked. Shallots are ideal for risottos and also delicious caramelized as a side dish.

Pickled Onions pickled in vinegar and spices will keep in the cupboard for a year.

Strung up Onions can be plaited by their dry stalks and hung up for storage; cut off and use as needed.

'Longor'

'Florence'

'Matador'

'Ambition'

Garlic

Make sure you leave space for this essential kitchen garden crop. Renowned as being one of the most pungent and aromatic of all the vegetables, garlic has a wonderful flavor and aroma. It is a key ingredient in cooking and is said to be beneficial to health.

Flowers Cut off most garlic flowers you see forming, leaving a few for dried flower displays.

Buying bulbs

Always buy certified virus-free stock from reputable suppliers and choose varieties suitable to your growing conditions. Don't plant supermarket bulbs, since they are imported and may be unsuitable for the climate.

Healthy cloves Discard any spindly, withered, or under-sized cloves as they won't grow into large bulbs.

Growing

Garlic requires a warm, sheltered, and sunny site with well-drained soil. It is a useful crop to grow, because it is planted in fall and grows through the winter, when the beds are otherwise empty. Garlic can also be planted in spring, although the bulbs produced will be smaller.

◆ **PLANT GARLIC** by breaking open the bulbs and pushing the individual cloves into the soil or in pots, leaving just their tip poking out above the surface of the soil or potting mix.

◆ **THEY CAN** also be started under cover in small pots to speed up their development, before planting out once they have produced strong growth. Cloves should be planted 6in (15cm) apart. Keep the area well-watered and free of competing weeds.

◆ **THE CLOVES** should swell into generous-sized bulbs with the fall-planted ones ready to harvest in early summer; spring-planted bulbs mature from midsummer onward.

Storing & Using

Garlic can be used in: sauces...stews... risottos...or can be slow-roasted...

Garlic stores well for up to nine months when dried and hung in a cool, dry place. It is invaluable for sauces with onions and tomatoes, and adds a tang to potato wedges. Try making garlic sauce, mixing it with bread crumbs, olive oil, and lemon juice, to serve with fish or chicken dishes.

garlic bu

Green onions

This is a quick and easy crop to grow that takes up little space and can even be raised in patio containers. Green onions add a fresh, mild-onion flavor to summer salads and Asian cooking, and there are many varieties to try.

Growing

Green onions prefer fertile, well-drained soil in full sun. They are raised from seed, usually outdoors, but can be started under cover, before planting them outside three weeks later, for an earlier crop.

◆ **SOW OUTDOORS** directly into shallow furrows that are ¾in (2cm) deep, in rows 12in (30cm) apart, leaving about ½in (1cm) between each plant. Green onions are very fast growing—during summer they can be ready within about five weeks after sowing.

◆ **GREEN ONIONS** are ready for harvesting when the stems are about ½–¾in (1–2cm) thick, and about 6in (15cm) tall. Use a hand fork to lightly pry them out of the ground, being careful not to disturb the remaining plants in the row.

◆ **SOW SEEDS** in regular batches for a prolonged harvest.

Storing & Using

They can be added to: salads...stir-fries...soups... Asian dishes...sauces...

Green onions don't store well, so only pull them when you need them. You can keep them in the refrigerator for a few days but they will soon spoil—and they cannot be frozen. Green onions are delicious chopped into salads and provide a more delicate flavor than ordinary onions in a wide range of dishes.

Routine care

Green onions are relatively trouble-free and very simple to grow. For a constant supply throughout summer, sow seeds every two weeks. They can also be grown through fall and winter under cloches and row cover, and even on windowsills. If you have a greenhouse, sow seeds into large containers, and enjoy a year-round supply.

Thinning out When seedlings are 3in (7.5cm) tall, thin out every other plant in the row to leave them spaced ¾in (2cm) apart.

Weeding Remove weeds regularly from around the seedlings to prevent them from competing for nutrients.

Watering Water regularly, and feed using a general-purpose liquid fertilizer as the plants mature.

green onion

Project
Onion & garlic drying rack

It is crucial that harvested onions and garlic have an opportunity to dry out in the sun and fresh air before you store them—they will then keep for longer. A drying rack will ensure that air can circulate freely around the produce and any dried soil can fall off.

step 3

MATERIALS & TOOLS

• wood, screwdriver, wire mesh, 8 L-shaped brackets, screws, hammer, staples

A work bench, clamps, and a cordless screwdriver will make the job easier, or you can work on an old table.

step 2

Hammer the staples along one side of the frame first, then pull the wire mesh taut before attaching the staples on the opposite side. Finish by attaching the mesh to the remaining two sides.

step 1

Galvanized L-shaped brackets make quick work of assembling the basic framework. Screw one bracket to each face of the corners using countersunk screws.

1 Start by making the frame that will support the wire mesh. Connect the four pieces of the frame using flat L-shaped brackets screwed into place.

2 Screw uprights to the sides and front edge of the frame to strengthen it and prevent the onions from falling off. The back edge will be attached to a fence.

3 Lay the wire mesh on the frame and secure it to all four sides with galvanized staples spaced approximately 8in (20cm) apart.

4 Hold the frame with its back edge against the fence and secure one corner through a fence post and the other through the fence rail with heavy-gauge screws.

step 4

Use a wood brace to hold the frame at the right height while you attach it to the fence. It can be removed after the front supporting legs are in place.

No fence

If you don't have a convenient fence or shed for supporting the rack, it will need four legs rather than two. Attach a diagonal wooden brace between each pair of legs to help keep the rack stable.

step 5

Make a small hole in the ground for each support before driving it in fully. This makes the job of getting the supports in the ground easier.

5 Drive a support into the ground at each front corner of the rack along the sides. With the rack perfectly level, screw the supports into place.

Always spread out your produce in a single layer so that the air can circulate through it more efficiently. Turning the produce periodically will also speed up the drying process.

Florence fennel & Kohlrabi

These slightly unusual vegetables are harvested for their swollen stems, and are very easy to grow. Florence fennel has a mild anise flavor, and is often used in stir-fries. Kohlrabi is part of the cabbage family, and has a mild, cabbagelike flavor. Both crops can be picked young and tender or left to grow for a more substantial harvest.

Timing Low temperatures can cause both crops, especially Florence fennel, to bolt, so don't sow them too early. Wait until the coldest weather has passed.

Sowing

◆ **TO SOW UNDER COVER**, sow two or three seeds into small pots during spring, then thin the seedlings when they are about 2in (5cm) tall to leave the strongest plant per pot. Plant them out in late spring, leaving 10in (25cm) between each kohlrabi plant; 12in (30cm) between the Florence fennel plants. Plants will require hardening off for a few days prior to planting out by putting them outside during the day, then bringing them back inside at night.

◆ **TO SOW OUTSIDE**, sow kohlrabi from early spring, Florence fennel from late spring, into furrows ¾in (2cm) deep. Sow the seed in small clusters, spacing the kohlrabi 10in (25cm) apart, and the Florence fennel 12in (30cm) apart. When the seedlings emerge, thin them out to leave the strongest plant per cluster.

Fennel tips

Take care not to confuse Florence fennel with the aromatic, leafy herb also called fennel. Florence fennel is an attractive plant to grow in the garden, and will develop quickly if given fertile, well-drained soil. Keep the area around the plants free from weeds that would compete for moisture and nutrients, and that may smother young plants.

Watering Water the plants regularly during the summer, and feed using a liquid fertilizer to promote strong growth.

Hilling up To blanch the stems and give them a sweeter flavor, pile soil up around the bulbs during summer.

Harvesting Harvest the stems by cutting through the base with a sharp knife. Plants can also be lifted whole and trimmed later.

Harvesting

The swollen stems of kohlrabi will take about 10 weeks until they are ready for picking, and should be no larger than a tennis ball. They should be cut at the base, at ground level, using a sharp knife. Florence fennel can be harvested at a younger stage, producing bulbs just 1½–2in (4–5cm) across in size, or when full-sized, at about 6in (15cm) across.

◆ **IF HARVESTING** in early summer, leave the stumps of Florence fennel in the ground and water them well. They will often resprout, providing more mini bulbs for the remainder of the growing season.

◆ **AFTER HARVESTING** kohlrabi, pull the roots from the soil and prepare the area for another crop.

Kohlrabi tips

Being part of the cabbage family, kohlrabi prefers heavy, rich soil that has been improved with plenty of organic matter. However, it is more tolerant of poorer soil conditions than many of the other cabbage relatives.

Cover up Watch out for pests, such as cabbage white butterflies and birds, which will quickly destroy the crop.

Weeding Remove competing weeds by hand, being careful not to disturb the swelling stems of the plant.

Harvesting Harvest the stems as soon as they are ready. Stems left too long become tough and inedible.

Storing & Using

Florence fennel can be used in: cheesy casseroles...salads...soups...
Kohlrabi can be used in: stews...soups...salads...stir-fries...

Both Florence fennel and kohlrabi can be stored in the refrigerator for a few days, or can be chopped, blanched, then frozen for up to 6 months. Florence fennel is good with cheese or fish, and can be eaten raw. Kohlrabi is lightly flavored and can be added to soups, stews, and stir-fries, or steamed as a side dish. The leaves can be eaten, too.

Florence fennel

white kohlrabi

Celery root & Parsnips

These two essential winter staples are perfect for supplying the kitchen with vegetables when the garden is at its least productive. Celery root has a mild, nutty flavor, and one of its main virtues is its longevity in storage. Parsnips will benefit from exposure to the frost before harvesting, because this makes them sweeter.

Sowing celery root

Celery root needs a long growing season in order for the stems to mature fully, so seeds should be started off under cover in early spring.

Planting out Harden the seedlings off once they reach a good size and plant them outside into their final location. Water them in well.

Watering Give the plants plenty of water and don't let the soil dry out. Celery root grows best in very moist soil.

Growing

◆ **CELERY ROOT IS OFTEN** thought of as a root crop, yet it is the large, swollen stems that are eaten. To produce these, celery root should be sown in early spring in small pots under cover, and planted out in late spring or early summer. Plant the seedlings 12in (30cm) apart and keep the centers of the plants just above the surface. It is an easy crop to grow, not minding sun or shade, although it does require a fertile soil.

◆ **PARSNIPS REQUIRE** a sunny open site, and soil that has been dug deeply to allow the taproots to develop and grow. Alternatively, grow them in a raised bed, where you can provide the deep, free-draining, rock-free soil they need. Seeds should be sown directly into the soil in shallow furrows. Once the seedlings emerge they should be thinned out to 4–8in (10–20cm) apart, depending on the size of parsnip roots desired.

Celery root Remove offshoots from celery root as soon as you see them, because these will compete with the main plant for nutrients.

celery root

Growing tips

Parsnips and celery root can be damaged by carrot rust flies burrowing into the roots. In gardens with bad infestations it is best to create a barrier to prevent the low-flying pests from landing and laying their eggs. Parsnip canker is a fungal disease causing black growths on the roots. Remove and dispose of infected plants immediately.

Seedlings Thin out parsnip seedlings when they emerge. Be patient, the seed can be very slow to germinate.

Watering Keep the plants well watered, particularly when they are young, because they can quickly wilt and die.

Carrot rust flies Watch out for carrot maggots on celery root and parsnips. Erect a mesh barrier to protect the plants from attack.

Routine care

Since celery root likes moist conditions, it will benefit from a thick layer of mulch placed around the plants in summer. Take care to keep it away from the stems. Regularly hand weed around plants, water regularly, and occasionally give them liquid feed.

◆ **IF YOU DON'T** require the space for planting something else in the garden, it is best to only harvest parsnips and celery root as and when they're needed, since they keep better when left in the ground. Both vegetables should be ready for harvesting in the fall and well into the winter months.

◆ **TO HARVEST** either vegetable, place a fork underneath the plant and gently pry it out of the ground. Be careful with parsnips since the long taproot can easily snap, particularly in heavy soil.

parsnips

Storing & Using

They can be used in: stews...or mashed...or to make chips...

Both vegetables will store in the refrigerator for a few days but are best pulled as you need them. Parsnips are good with beef, and baked celery root with parmesan cheese is delicious.

Parsnip chips For delicious, homemade munchies to serve with drinks, deep-fry a thinly sliced parsnip, drain on paper towels, and season with salt.

Parsnips in sand Remove the tops of the parsnips, bury the root in moist sand, and keep in a cool place, such as a shed or garage. They will store for 6 months.

Rutabagas & Turnips

Turnips are one of the most versatile vegetables in the kitchen and can be grown not just for their delicious roots, but also for their leaves, which can be used like cut-and-come-again salad greens. Sweet-tasting rutabagas are perfect for providing a delicious vegetable for late fall and winter dinners, when there is very little else growing in the garden.

turnip 'Purple Top Milan'

Rutabaga tips

Prior to sowing, prepare the soil thoroughly by digging in plenty of well-rotted organic matter, such as garden compost. Remove any large rocks that could cause the roots to fork, and rake the soil surface level.

Thinning To produce full-sized roots, rutabaga seedlings should be thinned. This can be done gradually, always leaving the strongest seedlings.

Protection Cover the seedlings over with fine mesh to prevent pests, such as cabbage white butterflies and birds, from attacking the crop.

Growing

◆ **RUTABAGAS ARE** sown directly in the soil to allow them to develop their roots without disturbance, from mid-spring to midsummer. They are particularly slow-growing, taking about five months from sowing to harvest. Sow the seeds thinly, ¾in (2cm) deep, in rows spaced 15in (38cm) apart. Thin out the seedlings as they develop to a spacing of 9in (23cm) apart.

◆ **TURNIPS CAN** be sown directly outdoors (see right), but can also be started under cover to extend the growing season. Fill small pots with potting mix, water well, and then sow two or three seeds in each, ¾in (2cm) deep. When the seedlings emerge, thin them to leave the strongest per pot. Harden them off on a porch or in a cold frame before planting them out, 4in (10cm) apart, with 12in (30cm) between each row.

rutabaga

rutabaga 'Ruby'

Routine care

Water seedlings regularly to encourage the roots to swell—if the soil dries out it can cause them to split. Turnips and rutabagas can be prone to flea beetles, so protect plants with fine mesh to prevent them from being damaged. Early-sown plants will need to be protected with row cover if cold weather is predicted.

◆ **BABY TURNIPS** are ready to harvest in as little as six weeks, and should be carefully pulled when they reach the size of a golf ball. The small roots are tender and sweet.

◆ **FULL-SIZED TURNIPS** can take up to 35 weeks to mature, depending on the variety, and are ready when the foliage starts to die back. To grow over a long period, harvest some young, leaving the rest to mature fully.

turnip 'Oasis'

◆ **CHECK THE SOIL** pH if growing rutabagas, since they are prone to clubroot, which is less prevalent in alkaline soil.

◆ **TENDER TURNIP** varieties will not survive the winter, so make sure they have all been lifted before the temperatures drop.

Storing & Using

They can be used in soups... stews...or can be boiled...or roasted...or mashed

Turnips and rutabagas will keep in the refrigerator for a week. Alternatively, dice, blanch, and freeze the roots, or cook, mash, and then freeze. When frozen, both will keep for up to 9 months. Rutabagas are traditionally served mashed, but are also delicious when roasted in the oven with herbs.

Mashed Boil and mash rutabagas with butter, a little salt, and some freshly ground black pepper.

Turnip soup Turnips are a good addition to soups, providing a mild flavor and lots of substance. Top with crunchy fried bacon.

Turnip tips

If you want to grow turnips for their young, tender leaves, harvest the foliage every few weeks from mid- to late spring. The plants will still form small roots, but they will develop slowly. When harvesting turnips grown only for their roots, lift them when they reach your preferred size. Hardy varieties can be left in the soil until needed, even throughout winter.

Sowing seeds Turnips should be sown outdoors in spring into furrows, ¾in (2cm) deep, spaced 8in (20cm) apart.

Weeding Regularly hand weed among the emerging seedlings, taking care not to disturb the developing roots.

Harvesting Harvest young turnips during the summer to enjoy their delicious flavor and succulent texture.

Beets

One of the most colorful root vegetables to grow, beets
are reliable and relatively trouble free. They are best known for
their round red roots, although there are also yellow, white,
and striped varieties—with slender, stumpy, or fat roots.
All taste delicious, especially when roasted to bring out their
natural sweetness, and, of course, when they are pickled.

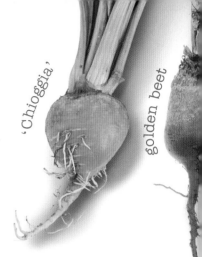

'Chioggia'

golden beet

Sowing inside

Sowing beets indoors gives
them a head start as long as
they are planted out before
their roots fill their pots or
cells. Sow from late winter.

Thinning Sow one seed in each
pot or cell. If more than one seedling
germinates, then thin them out to
the strongest one.

Planting Plant out the seedlings at
a spacing of 4in (10cm) between each
plant, taking care not to cause any
disturbance to the roots.

Growing

Beets require a moist, fertile, well-drained soil, and can be grown
in sun or light shade. Avoid growing them in rocky soil, which
can cause the roots to split. Unusually, the "seed" of most
varieties is more like a capsule, and usually contains three or four
true seeds. Thin the seedlings after sowing.

◆ **BEETS CAN** be prone to bolting if sown too early, meaning
that they run to seed. To avoid the risk when sowing outdoors
in spring, choose bolt-resistant varieties such 'Boltardy'.

◆ **ON SMALLER PLOTS** consider growing beets in large
containers and harvest them while young and tender.

Sowing outside

Seeds can be sown
directly outside
from spring to
midsummer.
Prepare the soil
before sowing by
digging it over,
removing any
weeds and rocks,
then rake the
surface level. The
seeds are large,
so are easy to
space out in rows.

Sowing Create a shallow
furrow, water it well, and sow
seeds at 4in (10cm) intervals.

Thinning One seed can
produce many seedlings so thin
out to leave the strongest.

'Green Top'

'Red Ace'

'Boltardy'

Growing tips

Beets are fairly maintenance free and grow with minimal intervention. However, a few routine jobs are worth doing.

Weeding Regularly hand weed between the seedlings to stop weeds from competing for moisture, taking care not to damage the roots.

Routine care

Beet plants will tolerate drought but they produce more succulent roots if watered well during dry spells. Don't overwater them, however, because this can encourage leaves to grow at the expense of the roots.

◆ **SOW REGULARLY** every two or three weeks throughout spring and midsummer to ensure a constant supply.

◆ **IN DRY SUMMERS**, mulch around plants to retain moisture.

◆ **HARVEST BEETS** about 12 weeks after sowing, although this depends on the variety. The roots taste at their best when dug up young and tender. Use a hand fork to gently pry the roots out of the ground.

Watering When watering, direct the flow to the base of the plants. Avoid wetting the leaves because this can encourage diseases to spread.

Storing & Using

They can be used in soups...salads... or can be roasted...or pickled...

Surplus beets can be stored in layers in wooden boxes lined with newspaper and filled with sand. Young beets can be frozen. Boil them until tender, slice or cube, then freeze for up to 6 months.

Soup Beet soup, or borscht, can be made in a variety of ways. In some countries it is traditional to add bacon or other meats, in others yogurt or sour cream is added.

Pickled Dice or slice beets for pickling and put in sterilized jars with vinegar, garlic, and bay leaves. They will keep for up to a year.

Harvesting Pick your beets while they are young, and eat them immediately to enjoy their tenderness and delicious flavor.

Radishes

One of the fastest and easiest of the salad crops to grow, radishes are perfect for beginners since they take just a few weeks from sowing to harvesting. They're ideal for filling small gaps in the garden, and can be sown alongside other slower-maturing crops.

Continuous crops Sow summer radishes little and often in spring and summer for a continuous supply of delicious, crunchy roots.

Sowing outdoors

Prepare the soil before sowing, digging it over to remove any weeds or rocks, then rake it level. Sow the seeds directly in the soil, in spring and summer for summer radishes, and late summer for winter varieties.

Preparing furrows Create furrows ½in (1cm) deep, spacing them 6in (15cm) apart for summer radishes, and 10in (25cm) apart for winter types.

Watering the seeds Before sowing, water the furrows, then sow the seeds about ½in (1cm) apart. Thin out excess seedlings as they emerge.

Growing

Choose between the two main types of radishes. Traditional summer radishes are very fast-growing, and can be sown and harvested from spring to fall. Winter and Asian (mooli) radishes produce larger roots than summer types, and are sown in late summer, ready to harvest from mid-fall to spring.

◆ **YOU DON'T** have to wait long to be harvesting these delicious crunchy vegetables. Summer radishes take as little as three to six weeks between sowing and picking. Winter radishes are slower to mature but they are well worth the wait.

◆ **DON'T LEAVE SUMMER** radishes in the ground for too long or they become woody, pithy, and inedible very quickly. Pick the radishes daily, checking along the row to find the largest roots. Pull them as soon as they are big enough.

radishes

Harvest Pull summer radishes out by hand or gently ease them out with a trowel. Large winter radishes should be lifted using a spade.

Jerusalem artichokes

Make sure you have plenty of space in the garden if you decide to grow these knobby root vegetables. Harvested in fall, these vigorous, tall perennials can also provide pretty yellow flowers in summer. Expensive to buy in the supermarket, growing Jerusalem artichokes is a cost-effective way to enjoy these sweetly succulent delicacies.

Flowers Jerusalem artichokes are related to sunflowers and will provide your garden with an impressive floral display during the summer.

Growing

If you have poor soil and an area of shade in the garden then don't despair, because Jerusalem artichokes will positively thrive in these conditions. They are the thugs of the vegetable world and will quickly swamp and shade out other plants if they're not kept in check. However, once you have tried these nutty-tasting tubers, you will agree that they are well worth including.

◆ **TUBERS SHOULD** be planted in early to mid-spring after digging over the soil and adding well-rotted manure or garden compost. They should be planted 6in (15cm) deep and 24in (60cm) apart. If you are growing more than one row, then space them 36in (90cm) apart.

◆ **THEY ARE** relatively trouble free and should be harvested as and when they are required in fall and winter. Harvest them as you do potatoes, by lifting with a garden fork.

Wind protection

Jerusalem artichokes are simple to grow but their tall, rampant habit can make them susceptible to wind damage. To help prevent this, mound the soil up around the base of each stem. Large clumps will withstand the wind better than individual plants.

Storing & Using

They can be used for: salads...or can be roasted...boiled...or braised in butter...

Tubers keep unwashed in the refrigerator for about 2 weeks, but are not suitable for freezing because they discolor and their texture deteriorates.

jerusalem artichokes

Plant supports On exposed sites it may be necessary to help to prevent wind damage by using stakes and strings for support.

vegetables

stems

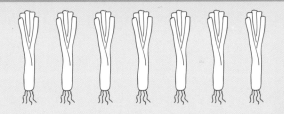

leeks • celery •
rhubarb • asparagus

Leeks

If you find onions strong and overpowering, try growing leeks for a milder flavor. Not only is this delicious vegetable easy to grow, but it is also an essential winter crop, providing flavorful sustenance from fall to early spring, when your choice of vegetables is more limited.

Storing & Using

They can be used for: soups ...stews...salads...quiches...

Refrigerate for up to 2 weeks. Frozen leeks become mushy, but you can use them in soups and stews for up to 3 months after freezing.

Sowing

To get leeks off to an early start, sow seeds under cover in a greenhouse or on a window ledge in midwinter.

Container sowing Lightly sprinkle seeds over moist seed-starting mix in seed flats or recycled pots. Leeks don't mind having their roots disturbed so can easily be lifted and transplanted.

Trim the roots Before transplanting, give their roots a quick trim. This makes it easier to drop the seedlings in their planting holes.

Growing

Leeks are best grown in seed flats under cover (see left), then transplanted to their final locations when they are about 6–8in (15–20cm) tall. Plant them out 8–12in (25–30cm) apart. They prefer full sun but will tolerate some light shade.

♦ **TO PLANT THEM OUT,** make holes 2in (5cm) wide and 6in (15cm) deep. Trim the roots (see left), leaving about 1in (2.5cm), then drop the plants into the holes. Don't push the soil back but instead water them in (see below), allowing the soil to crumble naturally around the plants. This allows space for the stems to swell.

♦ **MOUND SOIL** around the base as the leeks grow. The mounding is what will produce the blanched, white stems.

Puddle planting When planting young leeks out, make a hole and drop a plant in. Don't replace the soil but instead water well to create a puddle around the plant.

leeks

Celery

Traditionally, celery was considered one of the trickier crops to grow. It had to be planted out in a deep trench with the soil hilled up to keep the sun off the developing stems. This ensured nice white stalks of celery. Today's self-blanching varieties do the same job with far less trouble.

Storing & Using

It can be used in: salads… soups…casseroles… stuffings…stir-fries…

Good-quality, fresh celery is a treat. It can be stored in the crisper drawer of the refrigerator for a week or so and eaten with peanut butter or in a Waldorf salad, where it is one of the essential ingredients. Alternatively, you can cut celery into pieces, blanch it, and freeze it for up to 9 months, but it becomes mushy when defrosted, so frozen celery is best used to make soups or casseroles. Once made, these can be frozen if needed.

Seedlings Once the seedlings are big enough, they can be transferred to individual pots to grow on.

Growing

Although some consider the old, trenching varieties of celery to have a better flavor, beginners are advised to avoid them. After sowing under cover, plant out self-blanching seedlings 9in (23cm) apart in blocks (see below). Harden the plants off before planting out in well-prepared soil containing plenty of well-rotted organic matter, to help the soil retain moisture.

◆ **USE CARDBOARD** to wrap the stems on the outside of the blocks as they emerge from the soil. This will prevent the sun from reaching the stems and turning them green.

◆ **HARVEST FROM** August onward, making sure your crop is all harvested before the first frost arrives.

celery

Growing tips

Celery requires a long growing season, so start it off indoors in early to mid-spring, scattering the seeds lightly on a seed flat of moist potting mix. They require light to germinate, so cover plants with a minimal amount of mix, if any. Place in a heated propagator and pot them individually when they emerge. Plant them out when they are 6in (15cm) tall.

Plant in blocks Plant self-blanching varieties in a close grid. This will prevent the sunlight from reaching the stems.

Harvest carefully Celery lasts better if you keep the root intact when you harvest. Once cut, stems rapidly turn brown.

Rhubarb

This traditional kitchen garden perennial will reward you with a bumper crop of brightly colored red or pink stems from late spring to midsummer. Rhubarb is a hungry, luxuriant plant, so fertilize and water it well to keep it healthy and producing abundantly year after year.

Growing

Rhubarb requires a rich, heavy soil, so prepare the planting area well by digging it over and incorporating lots of rotted manure or garden compost. It is a large, long-lived perennial plant so consider the long term when deciding where to plant it.

- ◆ **HARVEST REPEATEDLY** in spring and summer by pulling and twisting the stems upward. Don't pick after midsummer to give the plant time to recover, ready for next year's crop. Stems that grow in late summer are also tough.
- ◆ **LARGE PLANTS** should be divided in the fall to encourage healthy growth, and to prevent the center from becoming woody. Keep strong, healthy sections and discard the rest.

rhubarb 'Victoria'

Storing & Using

It can be used in: jam...pies...cobbler...cakes... muffins...pickles...or can be frozen...

Cut stems will keep in the refrigerator for a few days, and last longer with their leaves still attached. The stems can also be sliced and blanched before freezing, and will last for 6 months. Always discard the leaves, which are poisonous.

Jam Rhubarb is often combined with ginger to produce a beautiful, jewel-like pink jam.

Growing tips

Buy rhubarb as a young plant but don't harvest the stems for the first year to help it establish more quickly. Plant new plants from fall to spring. Rhubarb can tolerate some shade, which is a good way to make use of these areas.

Forcing Stems can be forced by placing a cover over the plant in winter. The first stems produced are very sweet and tender.

Mulching Rhubarb should be mulched with organic matter each year in spring to help retain moisture in the soil.

Harvesting Pick stems every couple of weeks until midsummer. Leave some leaves each time, so the plant can grow.

Asparagus

This is a fine example of patience being a virtue because you can't harvest asparagus spears for the first two or three years after planting. However, once you have tasted these delicate spears smothered in melted butter, you will realize that it was well worth the wait.

Storing & Using

It can be used in: quiches... risottos...pasta dishes...or can be grilled...or steamed...

The spears can be stored in the refrigerator for a few days by standing their bases in a glass of water, refilling it daily. To freeze, trim the spears and briefly blanch them first. They can be frozen whole or chopped. One of the best ways to eat the new season's spears is steamed with melted butter, lemon juice, and freshly ground black pepper. They also go well with chicken, salmon, and pork.

Quiche Crisp pie crust, free-range eggs, mature cheddar, and asparagus spears make this quiche a special treat.

Growing

The most popular way of growing asparagus is by planting "crowns," which are young plants, usually sold bare-root. It is a long-term crop, and may grow in the same bed for up to 15 years, so prepare the soil thoroughly before planting. Remove any perennial weeds, and dig in plenty of well-rotted compost.

- ◆ **ASPARAGUS PREFERS** light, fertile, and well-drained soil. If the soil in your garden is poor, then consider growing it in raised beds.
- ◆ **HARVEST SPEARS** in the third year after planting, using a knife to cut the stems just below soil level when they are 8in (20cm) tall.

Growing tips

Asparagus is easy to grow, but check for bright red asparagus beetles that can damage and kill the stems. Pick them off or use a suitable insecticide. The ferny growth may need staking during summer, before dying back in the fall.

Planting Plant asparagus crowns 12in (30cm) apart. They are often planted in trenches with a mound in the bottom to set on.

Harvesting The spears can be cut for about 10 weeks, after which they should be allowed to grow to keep the plant strong.

Care Remove the attractive ferny growth at the end of each year, when it starts to turn yellow and die back.

vegetables

herbs

annual & perennial herbs
• shrubby herbs

Annual & Perennial herbs

You can grow a wide range of annual and perennial herbs to add scent to the garden and flavor to your home cooking. Not only do many herbs look attractive, but an added bonus is that there are numerous ways of storing your homegrown herbs for future use. You will never need to buy expensive, short-lived supermarket herbs again.

basil

Growing parsley

Parsley can be bought from garden centers, but the quality is better if you sow your own. Sow the seeds directly in late spring and then every few weeks during summer for a continuous crop. Cover plants with a cloche for overwintering.

Pest attack Watch out for carrot rust flies; parsley and carrots are related and both can be attacked by this pest.

Annuals

Annual herbs are easy to grow from seed and you can get a good crop even from a small space.

◆ **CILANTRO (CORIANDER)** that is grown for its leaves does best in partial shade. Sow it directly outdoors in spring and harvest it when the leaves are young and fresh. Use the leaves and stems in Middle-Eastern, Mexican, and Asian cooking.

◆ **BORAGE** is a stunning annual herb whose leaves have a mild cucumber flavor and can be added to salads. Be warned, it is a prolific self-seeder, so make sure you really want to grow it.

◆ **BASIL** is a half-hardy, scented herb that is grown as an annual and is often associated with Italian cuisine. Sow the seeds directly outdoors in late spring. Try growing the purple-leaved variety to add color to your garden plot.

◆ **PARSLEY** is a popular annual that is technically a biannual, but is treated as an annual. Used in Italian dishes, flat-leaf parsley has a stronger flavor, while curly-leaf parsley is more compact.

parsley

dill

cilantro

golden marjoram

Perennials

From low-growing creepers to large shrubs, perennial herbs look good growing in their own dedicated bed in the yard or dotted among other plants.

- **CHIVES** produce beautiful purple flowers and are perfect as a border around beds or for underplanting fruit trees. Plant them near carrots; their pungent smell (they are part of the onion family) confuses the carrot rust flies and reduces attacks.
- **TARRAGON** is a hardy perennial with upright branched stems. It is traditionally used to flavor chicken dishes and sauces.
- **FENNEL** is a tall, attractive perennial with ferny anise-flavored foliage that is an eye-catching addition to the herb garden.

Growing mint

There are more than 120 varieties of mint to try, including chocolate, ginger, and orange. All types of mint are extremely vigorous though, so you should plant it in a pot in the ground to prevent it from taking over the garden.

Storing & Using

They can be used in: soups...stews...risottos...drinks...bread...pasta dishes... herb teas... or frozen...or dried...or in home remedies...

Fresh herbs store well for up to 10 days wrapped in damp paper towels in an open plastic bag in the refrigerator. The leaves also freeze well (remove them from the stems first). Alternatively, air-drying is a good way to preserve herbs with minimal loss of flavor and quality.

Bouquet garni
A bundle of herbs tied in a muslin bag or with string, these herbs are used to flavor soups, casseroles, and sauces. It is discarded before serving the dish.

Air-drying fennel This is an excellent way to preserve fennel fronds for use in soups, sauces, and salad dressings throughout the year.

Comfrey fertilizer Comfrey is the ideal herb to grow if you want to produce a high-nutrient feed for plants such as tomatoes (see p.58).

chives

marjoram

tarragon

lovage

mint

Shrubby herbs

Many shrubby herbs are evergreen and will provide year-round interest for your yard. Individual plants such as bay or rosemary can be used as focal points for the center of parterres and vegetable beds, while lavender and sage look—and smell—terrific when edging pathways and planted around seating areas.

Herb parterre A shrubby lavender plant takes center stage in a herb-filled parterre edged with low, tightly clipped evergreen hedges (see p.86).

Herb lawns

The creeping habit of thyme and chamomile make them ideal for creating areas of scented herbal lawn. Avoid walking on them too often—they can easily show wear.

Scented lawn Plant small specimens 10in (25cm) apart into well-drained soil and they will quickly knit together to make an evergreen carpet.

In the garden

Most shrubby herbs thrive in light, well-drained soil. If your yard has heavy soil, then dig in plenty of coarse sand to counteract this. Be aware that many shrubby herbs can get large and quickly outgrow their space if they are not trimmed regularly.

◆ **TRAIN BAY** as a standard or pyramid to create a focal point in the garden. Alternatively, leave it to grow into a bush to screen unsightly areas such as the compost heap.

◆ **USE ROSEMARY** as hedging; some varieties can get quite large. Similarly, rows of lavender can be used as a low-growing hedge to give a formal structure to the yard and attract bees.

◆ **PURPLE AND TRICOLOR SAGE** add a splash of color and make an attractive feature for any yard. Hyssop, lavender, and rosemary all produce beautiful flowers, which add an extra ornamental quality to any space.

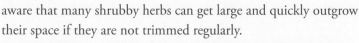

thyme

purple sage

green sage

Useful fillers

Herbs are extremely versatile and since they don't require a lot of nutrients, they can be slotted into spaces that are unsuitable for other plants. Use small herbs such as thyme and chamomile dotted along the edges of paths or even in the gaps between paving slabs.

Keep compact Lavender can be kept compact by clipping twice a year so it can fit into small spaces.

Fill the gaps Thyme plants can be used to fill tiny gaps in paths and at the edges, where it will slowly spread.

In pots

Herbs thrive in pots and these can be moved around as your design evolves, for example to provide an instant focal point. They don't need as much watering or feeding as most other plants in pots, but should be checked regularly throughout the summer.

◆ **PLANT A SELECTION** of herbs in the individual planting holes of a strawberry pot.

◆ **MOVE HERBS IN POTS** to a shady area to keep them from drying out when you are away.

Containers Herbs in terra-cotta pots make both beautiful and practical features in the vegetable garden.

Storing & Using

They can be used in: stocks...soups...fish dishes... or dried...or frozen...

Since rosemary and bay are both evergreen, you can pick the leaves as and when you need them. You can also preserve shrubby herbs by air-drying them. Tie them in small bundles and hang them up in a cool, dry place. When they are completely dry, store them in an airtight container. They will retain more flavor if you store them whole and crush the leaves when you are ready to use them. Dried herbs are best used within a year. As a guide, use one teaspoon of crumbled, dried leaves in place of one tablespoon of fresh herbs.

Soap Herbal soaps are easy to make with dried herbs and make great gifts for friends and family.

Oils and vinegars Add sprigs of herbs to oils and vinegars to make excellent infusions at a fraction of the price of those for sale in stores.

hyssop

rosemary

bay

FRUIT

Growing & Storing

fruit

soft

strawberries • a fruit cage • raspberries • a raspberry cane support • blueberries & cranberries • a sunken blueberry bed • blackberries & hybrids • gooseberries • currants

Strawberries

One of the nation's favorite fruits, these plants need little space and fruit freely, so they are ideal for smaller plots. They can be grown in hanging baskets hung on the garden shed, or in troughs and containers. Grow them in a raised bed to save on backbreaking weeding, and to make it easier to pick the soft, succulent, summer berries.

Netting Birds love these juicy berries so make sure you cover the plants early on with a net to protect them.

Planting

Dig over the plot thoroughly, removing all weeds, and add plenty of organic matter to the soil before planting. The best time to plant strawberries is late summer, while the soil is still warm. Water them in well after planting.

Spacing Plant strawberries using a trowel, spacing them 18in (45cm) apart, in rows 3ft (1m) apart.

Growing

Grow strawberries in well-drained but fertile soil, in a sunny, sheltered location. If you have poor soil, grow them in raised beds or containers instead. Always buy certified virus-free plants, and avoid planting in soil that has previously been used to grow potatoes or tomatoes. These crops are prone to the disease verticillium wilt, which can be passed to the strawberries.

◆ **STRAWBERRIES** establish better when planted in late summer, and will give a small crop the following summer. They can be planted in spring, although their first year's flowers should be removed to help them root better. Water new plants well.

◆ **GROW A MIX** of early- and late-season summer-fruiting varieties for sweet-tasting fruit from late May through to mid-July. Everlasting strawberries crop from midsummer to fall, although they aren't as tasty as summer varieties.

alpine strawberries

strawberries

Propagating

Strawberries constantly produce runners, which are shoots bearing new plants, making them easy to propagate. Stake the young plants into small pots of soil mix plunged into the soil. Keep them well watered, and after a few weeks, the stem between the new and old plant can be cut. If you don't want new plants, remove the runners to keep them from competing for nutrients.

◆ **IF YOU WANT** a constant supply of new plants, grow a few strawberry plants in a dedicated bed. Allow them to form runners and plant them out when large enough.

Anchor When a runner is sent out from the main plant, stake it into a pot of soil mix to encourage it to root quickly. It can be planted out once large enough.

Fruit protection

One of the key jobs when growing strawberries is preventing the fruit from coming into contact with the soil and rotting. There are various methods of keeping this from happening.

Plastic sheeting Planting through plastic sheeting or landscape fabric prevents the berries from rotting and also suppresses weeds.

Storing & Using

They can be used in: summer desserts... strawberries & cream...strawberry daiquiri... pies...strawberry salsa...milk shakes...ice cream...jam ...or can be frozen...

Eating your first bowl of strawberries with cream is the perfect way to celebrate the arrival of summer. Freshly picked strawberries don't keep for long in the refrigerator—a day or two at the most. Freeze for up to 12 months, although the fruit is mushy when defrosted, and is best used for jam-making or smoothies.

Jam An excess of strawberries can be put to good use in making a supply of jam for the pantry.

Collars These are placed around the plants, keeping the fruit off the soil. They can either be bought, or you can make your own using cardboard.

Summer pudding This quintessentially British dessert is easy to make, and is delicious served with ice cream.

Strawberry tart Make or buy a tart shell and fill with strawberries and other summer berries for a quick and easy dessert.

Milk shakes Fresh strawberries make the best milk shake ever. Combine with ice chips to make a slushie drink.

Straw This is the traditional method, hence the name "strawberries." Barley straw is the best type to use since it is soft and pliable. Buy it at pet shops.

Project
Fruit cage

It's important to protect the tasty fruit and vegetables that you've spent weeks striving to grow in your garden. Birds and small animals are unbelievably adept at knowing exactly when the time is right to steal your crops, so keep them at bay by making this simple protective cage.

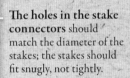

step 3

MATERIALS & TOOLS

- bamboo stakes or dowels in various lengths, stake connectors, garden netting, wire staples

To maintain a rigid structure that will withstand the rigors of repeatedly removing the netting when you harvest your produce, do not space the stakes more than 4ft (1.2m) apart.

step 2

The holes in the stake connectors should match the diameter of the stakes; the stakes should fit snugly, not tightly.

step 1

1 Drive four equal lengths of bamboo stake into the ground at a depth of about 8in (20cm) at each corner around the plant or plants to be protected.

2 Slide a stake connector on top of each stake. Most connectors have multiple holes so you can make a simple frame, as here, or join several stakes in a straight line to make a frame with longer sides.

3 Complete the assembly of the stakes, leaving enough room around the plant so that the netting, once it is in place, does not snag the plant.

4 Drape the garden netting over the structure, ensuring there is enough netting to enable you to stake it into the ground all the way around the cage.

step **4**

Wire staples, bent pieces of wire or short lengths of stake are perfect for holding the netting in place. The key point is that they can easily be removed.

Use small-gauge mesh to deter birds and make sure you replace it properly each time you access the cage.

This simple fruit cage leaves the plant or bush with ample room for further growth upward and outward. Make sure that the netting is held taut over the top and along the sides to prevent birds from becoming entangled in it.

Other systems

For bigger fruit and vegetable cages to protect established plants or bushes, there are plenty of alternatives to choose from. Some you can construct to suit your own specific requirements, using off-the-shelf components—aluminum tubing, frame connectors, and netting of the appropriate gauge. Others, such as fruit-tree cages, only require assembly. These alternatives are durable and long-lasting.

This large cage is made from commercial parts. Instead of removing the netting to harvest fruit, you can lift it or cut a hole in it, then tie it back together.

Metal hoops can be inserted into the ground in a row to protect plants that do not grow too high. Drape netting over the top of the row to form a tunnel.

Raspberries

Raspberries are relatively expensive to buy, but are very easy to grow and don't need a lot of space, which makes growing your own a good idea. They are one of the first berry fruits to crop each year, and taste wonderful when picked fresh. There are summer- and fall-fruiting varieties, which means you could be picking delicious fruit from midsummer to the first frost.

'Tulameen'

Raspberry canes

Raspberries can either be bought growing in containers, often with several plants per pot, or as wrapped bundles of bare-root canes (see below).

Buying Each plant comes as a single cane, a bit thicker than a pencil, with its own root system. Look for small white buds from which new shoots will grow.

Planting Prepare the soil well in advance with well-rotted compost or manure, and erect post-and-wire supports for summer-fruiting varieties. Space the plants evenly and water well.

Growing

Choose a sheltered site, out of strong winds but in full sun, since raspberries ripen best in these conditions. Plant container-grown plants at nearly any time of the year, but bare-root plants between late fall and early spring, unless the ground is frozen.

◆ **BEFORE PLANTING** the canes, dig a trench and add plenty of well-rotted manure or potting mix and combine with the soil. This helps to retain moisture.

◆ **SUMMER RASPBERRIES** require support, and should be planted next to horizontal wires, stretched 16in (40cm) and 32in (80cm) above the soil, between sturdy posts (see p.196).

◆ **RASPBERRIES** should be spaced 14–18in (35–45cm) apart and rows should be 4–6ft (1.2–2m) apart. They do not need planting very deeply, about 3in (7.5cm) is sufficient.

'Prelude'

'All Gold'

Routine care

Raspberries like free-draining soil, but they also need plenty of water. They will tolerate a little shade, but need plenty of sunshine to give the best yield.

◆ **KEEP PLANTS** well watered during the summer and apply tomato fertilizer to promote a good harvest. Mulch near the base of the canes to suppress weeds and retain moisture.

◆ **AS SOON AS** the fruit starts to ripen, protect it from birds. Cover the plants with netting, held taut using stakes to prevent snaring unsuspecting birds, or a cage. Fall-fruiting varieties seem to suffer less from attack by birds.

◆ **THE BERRIES** are ready to pick as soon as they turn fully red or yellow, depending on the variety, and pull away easily from the plant leaving the central plug behind.

Careful picking Pull the fruit gently from the plants to avoid damaging them, since they will keep for much longer when the fruit is whole.

Pruning

Summer- and fall-fruiting raspberries have different pruning needs.

Summer fruiting Old stems are pruned right after the last fruit has been harvested, right down to the base. Leave younger stems and tie them in.

Fall fruiting Prune in winter by cutting all stems down to the ground. New stems will appear in spring.

Storing & Using

They can be used in: jams...salads...cobblers...pies...smoothies...or frozen...

Extra raspberries are not to be greeted with despair. This fruit freezes incredibly well and can be used for plenty of desserts, including summer trifles, fruit salads, then, come fall and winter, spiced fruit chutneys, fruit cobblers, and mixed berry pies. If you don't have time to make jam when the fruit is ripe, simply freeze the berries and make the jam when you are less busy. Raspberries keep in the refrigerator for only a day or two, so are best eaten as soon as they are picked if you are not planning to freeze them.

Freezing Raspberries freeze very well, especially if frozen individually first by spacing them out on a tray. When they are frozen, they can be transferred to a plastic freezer bag and will not stick together, so you can use just a few at a time if you want.

Jam Raspberry jam is easy to make and there are dozens of recipes available. It will store for a year unopened. Once open, keep it in the refrigerator. Use it with yogurt, in pies, or as a sponge cake filling.

Project
Raspberry cane support

Most raspberry varieties benefit from being grown against a support. A relatively simple structure consisting of sturdy posts with taut wires running between them to which the canes can be tied in, it not only supports the plants and keeps them tidy, but also makes pruning and harvesting the fruit much easier.

step 3

MATERIALS & TOOLS

- four stakes, galvanized wire, four eye bolts, galvanized nails
- sledgehammer, drill, pliers, saw

step 2

step 1

Secure the bracing post with a single 4in (10cm) galvanized nail and drill pilot holes slightly larger than the diameter of the eye bolts.

Cut each bracing post at a 90-degree angle and use the cut end to help determine the position of the notch.

Drive in a bracing post alongside each of the main posts. This will be angled, so make sure that it will not obstruct the two supporting wires at the point where it will be attached to the main post.

1 Make two small holes in the soil approximately 16in (40cm) deep and your chosen distance apart, then hammer in the main supporting posts until they are completely firm in the ground.

2 Angle each bracing post, and where it crosses the main post, mark the main post for the location of the notch.

3 Cut a notch into the main post to fit the bracing post snugly, then mark and drill holes 16in (40cm) and 31½in (80cm) from the bottom of the main post.

4 Push an eye bolt through each of the holes, fitting a washer and nut to the outside of each post.

step 4

Figure-eight loop

The canes can now be tied in to the supporting wires with twine to stop them from being blown over or snapping. Use a simple figure eight—one loop of twine goes around the wire and the other around the stem of the plant. This method of tying in prevents rubbing but still allows enough room for the raspberry cane to grow.

step 5

5 Feed the galvanized wire through one bolt, use pliers to twist the cut end over the other, then feed the other end through its opposite bolt, maintaining good tension.

6 Using pliers, tightly wrap the other end around the taut wire and press the cut end firmly in place so there are no sharp wires protruding.

Using pliers, cut the other end of the galvanized wire to the correct length, allowing an extra 4in (10cm).

Add tension to each of the wires by tightening up the nuts on the eye bolts to take up any slack.

step 6

Position the raspberry cane support in a sunny or partly shaded location for best results. The support makes the task of picking the fruit much easier.

Blueberries & Cranberries

These closely related "super fruits" require moist, acidic soil—cranberries especially prefer boggy, wet soil. Few gardens are likely to offer these conditions, but they can easily be provided by creating raised or sunken beds, filled with lime-free, acidic potting medium.

Growing

The first step before planting either fruit is to test the pH of your soil using a simple kit bought from a garden center—see p.21, "Know your soil," for details how. Both fruit require a sunny site and should be kept moist at all times. They are usually sold pot-grown, and are best planted from fall to spring.

◆ **BLUEBERRIES** are self pollinating, so you only need one plant to produce a crop. However, they fruit better if other varieties are grown nearby.

◆ **PRUNE** blueberries in early spring by removing a third of the older wood at ground level.

◆ **WATER THE PLANTS** regularly using rainwater, for instance from a rain barrel. Most tapwater is too alkaline for these acid-loving plants.

Netting Place nets over the fruit bushes as soon as they start to ripen to stop birds from taking the fruit.

Suitable fertilizer Don't use traditional fertilizers when feeding blueberries and cranberries, since they can increase the soil's pH. Only use fertilizers designed for acid-loving plants.

Blueberry bed

These plants naturally grow on boggy land, and require similar conditions if they are going to thrive in the garden. Their two main requirements are moisture and acidic soil. To achieve this, dig a 12in- (30cm-) deep pit, as large as you need, and line it with punctured pond liner. Fill the pit with lime-free, acidic potting mix, which is suitable for these plants.

Preparing to plant Take the blueberry plant out of its container and then tease the roots out gently.

Planting Dig a hole and plant the blueberry in it at the same depth as it was in the container. Firm it in and water well.

Mulching Mulch around the blueberry with well-rotted, acidic material, such as composted bark or pine needles.

Harvesting

Blueberries are ready for harvesting in midsummer, when they turn from greenish-white to deep blue. The attractive white bloom on the berries indicates that they are ready to pick. Cranberries ripen during the fall, turning deep, glossy red when they are ready (see right).

Picking fruit Pick the ripe berries individually, taking care not to dislodge any unripe ones.

◆ **RIPE BERRIES** should easily detach from the plant but take care not to squash them. Damaged berries can't be stored.

◆ **CHECK BUSHES** regularly during summer because the berries will ripen at different times on the same plant.

Cranberries

These low-growing, creeping evergreen shrubs thrive in similar conditions to blueberries, requiring moist, acidic soil. They produce their attractive red berries later than blueberries, in the fall.

Ripe berries Cranberries start to ripen in early fall and keep well for a couple of months when left on the bush, unless eaten by birds first.

Storing & Using

Blueberries can be used in: pies...muffins... cookies...pancakes...yogurt...smoothies... Cranberries can be used in: sauces...jellies... chutneys...drinks...or can be dried...

Make delicious blueberry pies and freeze them, or freeze the fruit in bags to use later. Cranberries freeze very well or can be dried. To dry them, pour boiling water over the berries to burst the skins, freeze them on a tray, then place them in a warm oven overnight.

Cranberry sauce Once you've made your own, you'll never buy it again. It freezes very well and will keep for at least 6 months.

Freezing Freeze berries on trays, then when they are completely frozen transfer them to freezer bags. Keep for up to 12 months.

Sunken planter An old ceramic sink can be filled with lime-free, acidic potting mix and kept moist, making the ideal place for growing cranberries.

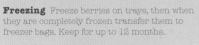

blueberries

cranberries

Project
Sunken blueberry bed

Blueberries are acid-loving plants, which means they must have acidic, lime-free soil. They also prefer soil that is free-draining but moisture-retentive. Unless your garden offers these conditions, the best way to grow a large number of blueberries is in a sunken bed, built in a sheltered, sunny or partly shaded site.

The frame should now set level and square in the hole, and just above the soil surface. The excavated soil can be used later around the edges.

step 2

step 1

MATERIALS & TOOLS

- treated wooden planks and stakes
- landscape fabric, acidic potting mix

Mark out the perimeter of the frame on the soil surface using the edge of a spade or a pointed stick.

Cranberries

Blueberries require plenty of space between plants, up to 5ft (1.5m), depending on the variety. To make full use of the bed, underplant the blueberries with cranberries, which also thrive in acidic conditions. These low-growing shrubs complement blueberries perfectly, and can bear surprisingly heavy crops.

1 Construct the frame of the bed in the same manner as the raised bed (see pp.38–39) and place it in position. Ensure the frame is square, using a T-square to check the angles, or by making sure that the diagonal measurements across the middle are equal.

2 Excavate the soil from within the outlines made (see above) and set it aside to use elsewhere. Dig down to a depth slightly less than the height of your wooden frame, so that the frame sets above the surrounding soil.

3 Secure the frame by driving in a wooden stake at each corner to 4in (10cm) deeper than the depth of the frame. If the frame is over 6ft (1.8m) wide, add further stakes to strengthen the sides.

step 3

Hammer in the corner stakes and ensure the frame is level. Use screws to attach the frame to the stakes, holding it in position if necessary.

step 4

Carefully cut the landscape fabric using a sharp knife or scissors, leaving it slightly larger than the frame itself. Lay the fabric in the frame and tuck the edges in neatly around the sides.

4 In order to contain the acidic potting mix, and to prevent deep-rooted weeds, lay landscape fabric in the bottom of the bed.

5 Fill around the outside of the frame with the excavated soil. The top of the frame should be slightly higher than the soil to keep lime from leaching into it. The bed is now ready for filling.

Pour in the acidic potting mix, level it, then firm it down. The mix should come to about 1in (2.5cm) below the top of the frame to make watering easier.

step 5

The soil must be kept moist, but not waterlogged, using rainwater and not tapwater whenever possible. A rain barrel may need to be kept just for this reason.

Blackberries & hybrids

These delicious berries are so easy to grow that one of the difficulties is keeping the plants' growth in check. There are lots of hybrids to choose from, including tayberries, loganberries, tummelberries, and the beautiful red-stemmed Japanese wineberries. Named varieties of blackberries are always sweeter and juicier than the wild ones found in fields.

Netting As the berries start to ripen, place nets over the plants to prevent birds from stripping off all the berries.

Growing

Despite their vigor, blackberries require a sheltered site if they are to fruit well, although they will tolerate poorer soil than most fruit and can be grown in light shade. Hybrid berries prefer better-quality soil. Prior to planting, construct a training system to enable you to tie in their rampant growth. Such a system need consist of nothing more than parallel, horizontal wires fixed 14in (35cm) apart to a fence or between two sturdy posts.

◆ **CONTAINER-GROWN** blackberries and hybrid berries can be bought and planted all year round, but it is best to avoid extreme hot or cold weather. Bare-root canes are only available from late fall to late winter. These should be planted out immediately to prevent their roots from drying out.

Planting

Whether you have chosen to plant bare-root canes or container-grown plants (see right), prepare the soil by digging it over thoroughly to remove any weeds. You should also enrich the soil before planting by digging in plenty of well-rotted organic matter. After planting, prune the canes back to 8in (20cm) above soil level and water well. Keep the plants well watered throughout the summer months.

Make the hole Dig out a hole, using the pot to determine the size of hole needed. Make the hole slightly wider than the root ball.

Remove the plant Remove the blackberry from its pot and gently tease out the roots from the root ball.

Position the plant Place the plant so that it is level with the soil and fill the hole using a 50:50 mix of soil and garden compost.

loganberries

tayberries

Routine care

Fruit develops on canes that were produced during the previous year's growing season. The canes can either be trained on a system of posts and wires or simply grown against a fence or shed.

Tying in Tie in new canes during the summer. It is these canes that will produce fruit for the following year.

Pruning Untie the old canes just after they have finished fruiting and prune them back.

Growing tips

Most blackberries and hybrid berries are very thorny, so take care not to damage your eyes and wear gloves when handling them.

◆ **MULCH AROUND** the canes with plenty of well-rotted manure in early spring.

◆ **PRUNE THE CANES** between late fall and early spring (see right).

◆ **TIGHTEN THE TRAINING WIRES** each year if they have become slack. Replace the posts if they have started to rot.

◆ **HARVEST THE BLACKBERRIES** when the fruit has turned black.

Harvesting
Pick carefully to avoid squashing the delicate berries.

Storing & Using

They can be made into: jams...pies...cobblers...or can be frozen...

All of these berries can be refrigerated for a few days and eaten fresh. You can freeze extras (perhaps to add to a smoothie later or turn it into jam). Alternatively, use the berries in a variety of desserts, some of which freeze well.

Blackberry & apple pie This traditional dessert has a sweet, tender crust and a melting, sweet-tart filling. Make it and freeze for later use.

Freezing These berries all freeze very well. Freeze them on trays, then transfer them to freezer bags. They keep for up to 12 months.

blackberries

Gooseberries

If gooseberries conjure up an image in your mind of tart-tasting, hairy green fruit, then think again. Gooseberries now come in a wide range of varieties and colors and, when left to ripen properly, can be one of the sweetest and tastiest of fruits.

'Hinnonmäki Red'

'Careless'

Growing

Gooseberries require a moist, heavy, fertile soil but will tolerate shade and can even be grown

Planting Add plenty of organic matter to the soil. Plant bare-root bushes to the depth of the soil mark on the stem and container-grown plants so the potting mix is level with the soil.

against a north-facing fence. They are usually grown as an open-center bush on a small, 8in- (20cm-) high trunk. However, they can also be trained as vertical cordons 14in (35cm) apart and 5ft (1.5m) tall or they can be fan-trained.

♦ **PRUNE BUSHES** twice a year. In winter you should prune them hard to reduce congested and crossing branches. In summer you should cut the new growth back to five leaves.

♦ **WATER GOOSEBERRIES** regularly during dry weather to avoid mildew. Place a net over the bushes as they ripen to prevent birds from stripping all the fruit off of the plants.

Harvesting Remove alternate, sour-tasting fruit in early summer and use for cooking. Leave the remaining fruit to ripen and eat fresh in midsummer.

Storing & Using

Gooseberries can be used in: jams...pies...
Currants can be used in: jellies...wines...sauces...

Keep gooseberries and currants in the refrigerator for a day or two, or freeze on trays and transfer to freezer bags, where they will keep for up to 12 months. Both fruits can be used to make a variety of delicious drinks, jams, and desserts. They also make good accompaniments to savory dishes.

Gooseberry cream
Add cooked berries to sugar and whipped cream for this dessert.

Currants

Packed full of vitamins, these berries come in a wide range of colors, from white through to pink, red, and black. All are easy to grow, which makes them ideal for beginners.

white currants

jostaberry

red currants

black currants

Growing

Red, white, and pink currants are grown in exactly the same way as gooseberries (see opposite), so they are suitable for growing as open-center bushes or fans and cordons on north-facing walls.

◆ **BLACK CURRANTS** have a different growing habit (see below) and require a bright, sunny location in heavy fertile soil.

◆ **PRUNE BLACK CURRANTS** in winter, using loppers to remove about a third of the older wood at ground level.

◆ **BIRDS LOVE** all currants, so place netting over the ripening fruit, pulling it taut to prevent birds from getting entangled.

◆ **JOSTABERRIES** are a hybrid between a black currant and a gooseberry, and produce large black, juicy berries. Resistant to gooseberry mildew, plant them 6ft (2m) apart.

Planting

Black currants are sold as "stools"—multistemmed bushes that send up new shoots from the base. Red, white, and pink currant bushes grow from a leg, or short stem. The different growing habits mean that the currants have different planting requirements (see right). Prior to planting, be sure to add plenty of organic matter to give the currants enough energy to enable them to produce lots of fresh new shoots.

Plant black currants deep Black currant stools are planted deeply to encourage new growth to shoot from below ground level.

Leave a "leg" Plant other currants so their "leg" is just above the surface of the soil. New growth emerges from the leg.

Water well Water plants in thoroughly, then mulch with well-rotted compost to retain water and suppress weeds.

fruit

trees & vines

apples • pears • plums, gages, & damsons • planting a fruit tree • cherries • peaches & nectarines • apricots • citrus & medlars • figs • quinces & mulberries • grapes & kiwis • melons

Planting

Apple trees can be planted all year round, but the best time is fall. The soil is still warm then and the tree can get properly established before starting into growth in spring.

Prepare a hole After preparing the ground thoroughly, dig a hole that is double the size of the root ball.

Planting Plant containerized trees at the same depth as in their pots; bare-root trees to the soil marks on the trunks.

Apples

With over 2,500 varieties to choose from, there is an apple to suit everybody's taste. Not only do apples reward you with delicious fruit in the fall, but they also provide a striking display of blossoms in the spring. Apple trees can be grown in the smallest of spaces and are even suitable for growing in pots and containers.

Growing

Dessert apples require a warm, sheltered site so their fruit will ripen fully, although cooking apples will tolerate some shade. There are various methods of training fruit trees for small spaces but two of the most popular are oblique cordons and espaliers.

◆ **OBLIQUE CORDONS** are single stems or trunks planted at a 45-degree angle with short branches or spurs along their length.

◆ **ESPALIERS** have a series of parallel, horizontal branches that are trained flat against a fence.

◆ **CHECK THE ROOTSTOCK** when selecting an apple tree for a small space. Certain rootstocks will restrict the tree's growth so it won't outgrow your space. The most suitable rootstocks are M27, M9, and M26. Ask at your local garden center for advice and details.

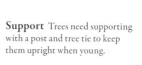

Support Trees need supporting with a post and tree tie to keep them upright when young.

'Golden Delicious'   'Cox's Orange Pippin'   'McIntosh'   'Fuji'   'Red Delicio

Pollination

Most apple trees require other apple trees fairly nearby to pollinate them. The trees should all flower at the same time so the bees can fly from the flowers on one tree to those on another. This ensures that the flowers will be pollinated and will set fruit.

Routine care

Cordons and espaliers should be pruned once a year in late summer by pruning back the new growth to one or two buds. Freestanding trees should be pruned in winter by removing crossing branches and dead wood. Keep the area around your apple trees free of weeds and water during dry periods.

◆ **THIN THE FRUITLETS OUT** in midsummer, reducing the clusters to one or two apples. This will ensure that those that remain will grow to full size.

◆ **HARVEST EARLY VARIETIES** in late summer, and late varieties in late winter.

Picking fruit
Harvest the fruit by gently cupping it in your hand and giving it a slight twist.

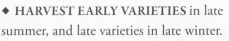
'Bramley'

'Ribston Pippin'

Storing & Using

They can be used in: pies... applesauce...chutneys... cobblers...or stored... or frozen...

Late apples store very well, either wrapped in wax paper in crates or loose in sacks. Make sure the fruit is not damaged though, or it will rot. Early varieties will only keep for a short time. If you have extra apples, you can cook them gently and freeze for use in winter to make pies or cobblers, or you can make apple juice and applesauce.

Store Late apples are the only ones worth storing. A cool shed or basement, where the humidity is low is the ideal place.

Chutney Apple chutney has a tangy, sweet flavor and goes very well with cheeses such as Cheddar, Cheshire, or white Stilton. It also complements ham or chicken dishes.

Apple pie This is a traditional, comforting dish, often served with whipped cream or ice cream. The combination of sweet, flaky pastry and spiced fruit is unbeatable.

Pears

Pears have an unfair reputation for being tricky to grow, but in fact they are just as easy as apples. They have a delicious, soft buttery texture and a sweetness that is hard to beat. You can grow them in small spaces—some varieties are even suitable for containers—and their pure white springtime blooms are a lovely sight to behold.

Fertilizer

Pears are hungry plants and benefit from a general-purpose granular fertilizer sprinkled around the roots in spring. Mulch afterward with garden compost or manure.

Containers Pears make beautiful specimens in containers but will need watering daily during summer. Make sure the container is cold-resistant and repot into fresh soil mix every couple of years.

Growing

Pears require a warm, sheltered site with well-drained soil and full sun in order for their fruit to ripen fully. Because they flower early, they can be susceptible to spring frost, so planting them in a sheltered site is especially important.

◆ **PEARS REQUIRE** a rich soil, so prepare it before planting by digging in plenty of organic matter. Plant trees that have a dwarf rootstock (usually Quince A or C) to restrict the size. They can be grown as cordons or espaliers (see p.208).

◆ **FLOWERS MUST** be pollinated before they can set fruit. If there are no pear trees nearby, you will need to plant at least two varieties that flower at the same time.

'Bartlett'

'Joséphine de Malines'

'Concorde'

'Doyenné de Comice'

Routine care

Cordons and espaliers should be pruned at the end of summer by reducing the new growth to one or two buds. Freestanding trees and trees grown in containers should be pruned when the tree is dormant in winter. Do this by thinning out any congested and crossing branches.

◆ **THIN EACH CLUSTER** of pears out in midsummer to prevent overcropping and to allow the remaining fruit to ripen fully.

◆ **PROTECT SMALL** young trees by covering them with row cover whenever frost is predicted.

Harvest Pears are ready to harvest from late summer to fall. Pick them when they are slightly underripe and leave to ripen indoors.

Growing tips

Pears are relatively easy to grow and once planted should be easy to maintain. Keep the area around the trunk free of weeds and prune once a year.

Pear drop "June drop" is a natural process that allows the tree to shed excess fruitlets. Do not thin the pears until after this has occurred.

Watering Young trees need watering every few days during dry periods. They must not dry out when in flower or fruit.

Storing & Using

They can be used in: pies...cobblers... salads...cakes...relishes...or pickled... or stored...or frozen...

Pears can ripen rather suddenly, so once picked, keep an eye on them. Store later varieties in wax paper, like apples (see p.209). They will keep for a few months. To freeze, choose ripe but not overripe fruit, peel and quarter, dip in water with a little lemon juice, then drain and dip in hot syrup. Freeze in the cooled syrup for up to 9 months.

Pear tart This makes an elegant dinner-party dessert. Pears also lend themselves to cakes and relishes, to being poached in wine, and to being used raw in summer salads.

'Conference'   'Blake's Pride'   'Beurré Hardy'   'Kosui'

Plums, Gages, & Damsons

These soft, juicy fruits with their beautiful, translucent skin are the quintessence of summer. They are easy to grow, requiring minimal pruning, and they often provide bumper crops, which is extremely rewarding. Plums and their close relatives, the gages, are one of the sweetest and most delicious fruit when freshly picked from the tree, while damsons, which are smaller, make the best jam imaginable.

'Merryweather Damson'

Growing

Plums require a warm, sunny site with free-draining soil. Because their early-spring blossoms can be susceptible to frost, choose a sheltered site. They thrive in rich, fertile soil so add plenty of organic matter before planting.

◆ **PLUMS CAN BE FAN-TRAINED** against a fence or trellis or they can be grown as a freestanding tree. They are not suitable for growing as cordons or espaliers.

◆ **'PIXY' ROOTSTOCKS** are usually used for growing plums. These will restrict the overall size of the tree.

◆ **MOST PLUM VARIETIES**, such as 'Victoria', are self-pollinating. That means only a single tree is needed, which is ideal for small gardens.

Trees in pots Plums will thrive in a pot but ensure trees have adequate drainage and can be watered once a day during dry weather, especially in summer.

Thinning Fruitlets should be thinned out in early summer to 2–3in (5–8cm) apart. This allows the remaining fruit to ripen fully.

'Cambridge Gage'   'Blue Damson'   greengage   'Victoria'   'Opal'

Planting

A healthy tree will reward you with fruit for at least 25 to 30 years, so it is worth preparing the soil well prior to planting. Thoroughly dig over the planting area, breaking up any layers of dense soil, often found just below the topsoil. This soil layer is largely impervious to water and so can restrict the growth of the trees.

Prepare a hole Dig a hole and plant the tree at the same depth as it was in its pot.

Fill Backfill the hole with a 50:50 mix of the original soil and good garden compost.

Water Attach the tree to a sturdy stake using a tree tie and water it in thoroughly.

Routine care

These fruit trees should only be pruned during the growing season. Avoid pruning them in winter since this makes them susceptible to diseases such as silver leaf and bacterial canker. Generally, it is best to prune plum trees as little as possible. Aim just to remove diseased, damaged, or crossing branches.

◆ **PROTECT THE BLOOMS** on young trees by wrapping them up in row cover when springtime frost is predicted, but remove the cover during the day to give access to pollinating insects.

Harvesting Pick plums when they feel slightly soft to the touch. They ripen at different times on the same tree, so check the fruit regularly. Leave the stem on the fruit when you pick it.

Storing & Using

They can be used in: jams... cobblers...pies...or frozen...

Plums, gages, and damsons do not keep for long, so they should be eaten, preserved, or frozen for later use. They develop their flavor best while on the tree, so pick them when they are ripe and ready to eat. They keep for a few days in the refrigerator or can be frozen on trays, then transferred to freezer bags. They will keep in the freezer for up to 6 months.

Chutney Plum chutney will keep for up to 6 months. Plums also make delicious jam, while damsons are used to make damson "cheese"—a dense, flavorful preserve.

Cobblers Plums, gages, and damsons all make delicious cobblers. If you prefer tart flavor, use damsons.

'Santa Rosa'

mirabelle

'President'

Project
Planting a fruit tree

Planting a fruit tree in the garden will create interest and structure on the plot and, of course, provide you with delicious fruit. Before planting, check that the mature tree isn't going to cast too much shade on your own—or your neighbors'—yard. Ensure the tree you are buying won't get too big and is a variety that you like.

Hammer the stake in prior to planting to avoid damaging the roots later on.

Bare-root trees

These are available when the trees are dormant and have finished growing for the year, usually between mid-fall and late winter. Plant bare-root trees immediately after buying them. If that isn't possible, plant them into large pots as a temporary measure.

MATERIALS & TOOLS

- fruit tree, potting mix
- spade, tree stake, tree tie, sledgehammer, galvanized nail

step 2

step 1

Year-old trees These are referred to as maidens. Those with branches are called feathered maidens; those without are known as maiden whips.

Lay a spade across the hole to ensure the tree is planted to the same depth as it grew at the nursery. Look for the soil mark on the trunk.

1   Dig a hole and ensure that the tree will be planted at the right depth, which is the same level as the soil mark on the stem.

2   Drive in a sturdy wooden stake to a depth of about 24in (60cm) into the soil to support the growing tree.

Check that the graft union, a harmless bulge in the trunk, is above the level of the soil.

Add potting mix to the soil from the hole at a 50:50 mix before backfilling. Firm the soil around the tree by lightly treading it in.

Attach the tree to the stake with a tree tie. Use a galvanized nail to prevent the tie from slipping down the stake.

3   Replace the tree in the hole and fill it with soil. Make sure the soil settles fully around the roots, leaving no air pockets.

4   Firm down as you backfill the planting hole, but try not to compact the soil.

5   Support the tree, using a cushioned tree tie to keep the tree from rubbing on the stake.

Water well, then spread a mulch of well-rotted compost around the base of the tree.

Container-grown cherry trees can be planted at any time of year, but bare-root trees are only available from January to April and should be planted as soon after purchasing as possible.

Hole depth Plant containerized trees at the same depth as in their pots; bare-root trees to the soil marks on the trunks.

Fill Backfill the planting hole and add compost and controlled-release fertilizer to the root area.

Stake Attach the tree to a stake using a tree tie. Water the plant well after planting to help it get established.

Cherries

A cherry tree dripping with luscious red fruit is not only a mouth-watering sight, but is a match for any ornamental plant in terms of beauty. And you do not need a huge yard to grow cherries; today, there are cherry trees for small yards, too. Enjoy sweet cherries fresh from the tree and use sour cherries for cooking.

Growing

Sweet cherries require a warm site to ripen fully, while sour cherries will tolerate shady conditions and can even be fan-trained on north-facing fences. Cherry trees no longer require an orchard to thrive, since recently developed rootstocks restrict size and vigor, making it possible to grow cherries in smaller spaces and gardens. They can be grown as freestanding trees on dwarfing rootstocks such as Colt or Gisela 5.

Row cover Protect the cherry blossoms in spring if frost is predicted, to ensure a crop of cherries in the summer.

◆ **MOST MODERN** cherry varieties are self-pollinating, meaning that you only need one tree. Others will need a second tree for pollination. Check the label before purchasing.

'Bing'

'Rainier'

Routine care

Prune both sweet and sour cherries when they are in leaf. Avoid pruning in winter or when it is raining since this can spread diseases such as silver leaf and bacterial canker. Prune sweet cherries minimally, only shortening overlong stems. Prune sour cherries by cutting a quarter of the branches that have fruited back to the next branch. Remove dead or damaged growth.

◆ **WATER YOUNG TREES** weekly during the summer months for the first couple of years. They will also benefit from an annual general-purpose granular feed in early spring, followed by a generous mulching with garden compost around the trunk.

◆ **WEED AROUND** the base of young trees to prevent the weeds from competing for nutrients. Protect small trees from frost while flowering by draping row cover over their branches.

◆ **USE SCISSORS OR PRUNERS** to harvest the cherries, leaving the stalks attached to the fruit.

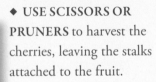

Harvesting Hold the cherries while you harvest them to prevent the fruit from dropping to the ground and spoiling.

'Morello'

Netting

Birds can quickly strip a tree of its sweet red fruit in a matter of hours. Place netting over small trees, using stakes or poles with the netting draped over the top. Stakes must be tall enough to clear the tops of the trees.

Stake down Secure the netting firmly along the ground with tent stakes to keep birds from sneaking underneath it.

Storing & Using

They can be used in: pies...jams...sauces...cakes...or preserve in brandy, vodka, or rum...or pit and freeze...

The cherry season is relatively short so make the most of them while you can. They will keep in the refrigerator for up to a week in an open plastic bag, but they also freeze well and will keep in the freezer for up to 12 months. To freeze, remove the pits (see right), lay them out on a baking tray until they are frozen, then pack them in plastic bags and return to the freezer.

In brandy Cherries in brandy are a tasty pantry treat, great for cooking, baking, or simply spooning over ice cream.

Pitting Removing the pits of cherries before freezing them means you can easily use the thawed fruit in desserts and sauces without having to worry about the pits. There are plenty of cherry-pitting gadgets on the market these days that make the job relatively quick and easy.

Peaches & Nectarines

These two delicious fruits are basically the same and have the same growing requirements. Many modern varieties do not take up much space and, being self-pollinating, you only need one tree. Peaches and nectarines are easier to grow than you may think and should reward you with a good crop of luscious fruit.

Protection The delicate spring blossoms need protection from harsh frost. If the blossoms are destroyed, all chance of fruit is lost.

Pruning Peaches and nectarines fruit on growth produced the previous year, so prune in summer to remove the wood that has just produced fruit.

Growing

Peaches and nectarines require a warm, sunny site protected from harsh frost and are usually grown on south-facing slopes or against fences.

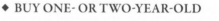

◆ **BUY ONE- OR TWO-YEAR-OLD** pot-grown trees from garden centers or online and check that they have been grafted onto dwarf rootstocks.

◆ **ALWAYS PRUNE** when the plant is in growth. Avoid pruning in winter because open wounds are susceptible to disease.

◆ **COVER THE PLANT** with row cover during winter and early spring to protect it from peach leaf curl. Protect the flowers with row cover when frost is predicted.

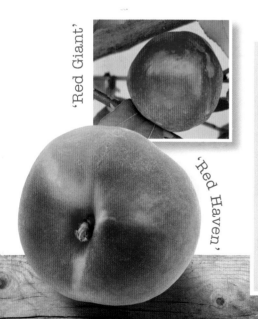

'Red Giant'

'Red Haven'

Thinning

Like most fruit with pits, peaches and nectarines need to be thinned out in summer, leaving the remaining fruit to ripen fully. If you fail to thin, the branches can snap from the weight. Also, overcropping in one year can result in no fruit at all the next.

First thinning When the fruit are the size of hazelnuts, thin to 4in (10cm) apart.

Second thinning Thin to a final spacing of 8in (20cm) when the fruit are walnut-sized.

Apricots

Closely related to peaches, apricots can be tricky to grow but the new, later-flowering apricots are less susceptible to spring frost. Choose a dwarfing variety to save space in the garden. Growing your own is well worth the effort; once you've tasted your own, store-bought ones simply won't do.

Growing

Apricots grow best when trained as fans against south-facing walls and fences, although they will also ripen when grown as freestanding trees on very sheltered, favorable sites. Either way, they require a rich, heavy soil and full sun.

◆ **PLANT TREES** in spring or late fall and keep them well-watered during their first year after planting.

◆ **FAN-TRAINED TREES** must be tied to a system of parallel rows of horizontal wires.

◆ **PROTECT THE BLOSSOMS** with row cover when frost is predicted.

Storing & Using

They can all be used in: sauces...purées...sorbets...cakes...cobblers...pies...compotes...

Peaches, nectarines, and apricots are delicious eaten straight from the tree, but they can also be refrigerated for a few days or frozen for up to 12 months. To freeze, remove the pits, poach the fruit lightly in a sugar solution, then cool and freeze in the liquid.

Preserving in brandy All stone-fruit can be preserved in alcohol and will keep for 12 months.

Making jam Peaches, nectarines, and apricots all make delicious jam that will keep for 12 months. You must add pectin for the jam to set.

Wasp trap Hang wasp traps around the tree to prevent wasps from destroying your treasured crop of apricots.

apricot

Training & pruning

Apricots, like all members of the pitted fruit family, should be pruned when in full growth. If you prune them in winter, the open wounds make them susceptible to silver leaf (see p.236) and canker (see p.234).

Pinch off shoots In springtime, pinch off overcrowded young shoots to leave a space of about 4in (10cm) between each one.

Tie in shoots In midsummer, tie some of the young shoots to the support. These will provide the structure and fruit for the following year.

Trim new growth In late summer, use pruners to cut some of the new growth back to about three leaves.

Citrus & Medlars

Citrus plants should be grown under cover in cooler climates but their benefits include attractive, evergreen foliage, scented flowers, and fruit all year round. Medlar trees are fully hardy and provide a wonderful ornamental feature, with their beautiful blossoms and quirky-looking fruit that are perfect for jelly and jam making.

Medlars Looking like a cross between an apple and a rose hip, medlars must be nearly rotten before they can be eaten.

Medlar flowers Their pretty pink-tinged flowers make medlars worth growing for their ornamental qualities alone.

Growing

◆ **WHEN BUYING CITRUS** trees, look out for hardier varieties. Most require year-round protection in an enclosed area but Meyer lemons and kaffir limes are worth trying outside. Grow citrus trees in pots, then you can remove them from the polytunnel during warm spells. Wrap tender citrus plants in row cover during cold periods, even if you are growing them in a polytunnel. Prune the trees lightly to remove diseased or dead branches and harvest the fruit when it is soft and smells fragrant.

◆ **GROW MEDLARS** as small trees or bushes—choose varieties that have been grafted onto quince rootstocks to restrict their size—and dig in some well-rotted manure or compost before planting. Being self-pollinating, you only need one specimen. Medlars prefer a warm, sheltered site but will tolerate some shade. Prune in winter as you would an apple tree, but keep the pruning to a minimum once the tree is established. Mulch young trees each spring and feed with a general fertilizer.

Storing & Using

They can be used for: jam ...preserves...jellies...cookies ...drinks...cakes...pies...

Citrus fruit will keep in the refrigerator for a few weeks but keep longer on the tree. Medlars must "blet," or break down, until sweet-tasting. To do this, leave them on the tree or store them in sawdust in a cool, dark place.

Lemon curd Keep this treat refrigerated and use within 2 weeks of making.

Pickled lemons Used in Middle-Eastern and Moroccan cooking, these can be refrigerated for up to 6 months.

lime

lemon

Figs

Despite their balmy Mediterranean image, figs are hardier than you may think and can survive cold temperatures. The difficulty is getting them to produce ripe fruit. In warmer climates they will produce two crops a year; in cooler countries, you can only expect one.

Restrict roots Plant in a slab-lined hole to restrict the tree's root system and stimulate fruit production.

Growing

Figs require a warm, sheltered site in full sun. They are usually grown as fans on south-facing fences or as standards in pots.

◆ **PRUNE IN SPRING** or late summer by cutting out some of the older wood and leaving the new shoots. You can prune fig trees back hard if they have become too big and straggly.

◆ **PROTECT WITH ROW COVER** during winter if the tree is small enough. Pot-grown figs can be moved to sheltered spots such as porches or sheds if very cold weather is predicted.

◆ **HARVEST THE FIGS** when they are soft and start to droop.

Storing & Using

They can be used in: cakes...desserts...preserves... cookies...salads...

Ripe figs spoil quickly so eat them as soon as you pick them or keep them for a few days in the refrigerator. Fig jam is delicious and hard to find, so why not use the crop to make some? You can also freeze figs whole; they will keep for up to a year.

Dried Figs can be dried in a low oven until sticky and sweet. Enjoy them stuffed with roasted almonds or serve them with goat cheese and red wine.

Savory Fresh figs work in savory dishes as well as sweet. Try them with ham or blue cheese.

fig

Routine care

The trick to getting figs to produce fruit is to restrict their root system. Either grow them in pots or in 24in (60cm) planting holes lined with patio slabs. Plant them either in spring or fall.

Remove fruit in fall Unripe figs larger than the size of a pea should be removed in fall because they won't survive through the winter.

Prune at the base Figs may produce suckers at the base of the trunk. These should be removed with pruners as soon as they appear.

Fall drop Don't panic if a lot of figs fall from the tree in early autumn. This is the tree's way of ensuring that the remaining fruit matures.

Quinces

One of the more unusual fruit to grow, quinces bear beautiful flowers in spring, followed by large, yellow, pear-shaped fruit that ripens in fall. These are too hard to eat raw but are delicious when cooked. Quinces become a small- to medium-sized tree, and may take several years before cropping heavily.

Blossoms Quince trees produce beautiful white or pink flowers in mid-spring, providing a splash of color in the yard.

Storing & Using

They can be used in: jellies... jams...preserves...pies... puddings...chutneys

Quinces are a wonderfully aromatic fruit and store well. Place undamaged fruit on shallow trays and store in a cool, dry, and dark place. Ensure they are not touching. They will keep for up to 3 months. Quinces can only be eaten once cooked.

Quince cheese This is a preserved quince purée, best served with cold meats and cheeses. It keeps in the pantry for up to a year.

Growing

Quinces prefer fertile, well-drained soil in a warm, sheltered site. Their early flowers can be damaged by frost, meaning no fruit, so don't plant them in frost pockets. The trees can reach a height of about 12ft (3.5m), so choose a site that gives them room to grow, and consider the shade they will cast. Quinces are self-pollinating but fruit better with a second tree nearby.

◆ **WATER TREES** planted recently during any dry periods.

◆ **FRUIT DEVELOPS** singly at the tips of the previous year's growth and should be left on the tree for as long as possible, and picked before the first fall frost arrives.

◆ **TO PRUNE,** remove and thin out of some of the older wood to encourage new shoots that will fruit in their second year.

Feature Quinces can produce an abundant crop of fruit in fall, creating an attractive feature for the corner of the garden.

Mulberries

These trees are grown for their delicious, sweet, raspberry-shaped berries, which are widely regarded as something of a luxury. Growing to 30ft (10m) tall, however, mulberries are only suitable for larger yards, and can take up to eight years before fruiting.

mulberries

Growing

Mulberries like moist but well-drained soil in a warm, sunny, and sheltered site. They are self-pollinating, so only one tree is needed to produce a harvest. Plant trees in late fall or early spring.

◆ **MULCH YOUNG** trees with well-rotted manure around their base. Give them a general-purpose granular fertilizer each spring.

◆ **PRUNE LIGHTLY** since the wounds will bleed readily and don't heal quickly, leaving them prone to infection. If necessary, prune in winter, removing damaged or crossing branches.

◆ **HARVEST FRUIT** when fully ripe from late summer to early fall. Handle the berries carefully because they are easily damaged, and the juice can stain fingers and clothing.

Storing & Using

They can be used in: jellies... jams...preserves...pies...or can be used to flavor gin...

Mulberries are best eaten or cooked as soon as they are picked, although the berries will keep in the refrigerator for a few days. The soft fruit is not suitable for freezing since it turns to pulp when defrosted. Pies made with mulberries freeze well.

Mulberry jam The berries can be used on their own to make jam, or mixed with other fruit, such as apples, strawberries, and raspberries, for a pleasing new flavor.

Wine Mixed with grape juice concentrate, then allowed to ferment and age, mulberry wine is a treat.

Black or white?

There are two types of mulberry commonly available, with either black or white fruit. Although both produce edible berries, black mulberries are far tastier, while a white mulberry is best grown as an ornamental.

White mulberries These are grown for their decorative qualities, and have historically been used to feed silkworm caterpillars for silk making.

Black mulberries These are the ones to grow for their fruit, producing dark, juicy berries with an intense flavor that is hard to beat.

Grapes

'Concord'

If you have ever dreamed of producing your own wine, then having a garden gives you the opportunity to try. Wine grapes are climbing plants and can be accommodated in small outdoor spaces as long as they have room to climb upward. Dessert grapes are less hardy, but if you are lucky enough to have a greenhouse, they are just as easy to grow.

Growing in a garden Grapes are easy to grow but you should give them a high-nitrogen fertilizer in winter and water newly planted vines in dry weather.

'Chardonnay'

Growing

Wine grapes require a sunny, sheltered site to ripen fully. Fortunately, they aren't too fussy about soil type—after all, they grow in soils ranging from the extensive soil diversity in the Napa Valley to the shallow, flinty, alkaline soil found in the Champagne region of France.

◆ **CREATE A MINI-VINEYARD** on your plot by planting the grapevines 3ft (1m) apart in rows and with 5ft (1.5m) between each row. Plant the vines in early spring.

◆ **GRAPEVINES ARE CLIMBING PLANTS** so they need a system of horizontal parallel wires for their tendrils to cling to. They can also be trained up pergolas and arches or as a screen to create shade and privacy in the yard.

Pruning

Grapevines are rampant growers and need a regular winter pruning to keep their growth in check and maintain a neat and tidy appearance. You can also give them a light trim in summer—prune their new growth back to about five leaves.

First prune After planting, prune vines back to 12in (30cm) above soil level.

Mature prune With vertical cordons, prune the new growth back to two buds in winter.

Thinning

You don't need to thin individual wine grapes since they are small and form tight, close bunches that can easily be crushed for winemaking. However, dessert grapes do benefit from this rather laborious process because it helps the remaining fruit to develop to its full size and optimal sweetness. Thinning also protects the branches from splitting under the weight of the fruit.

Tiny buds Tiny buds appear prior to flowering. Keep the bunches dry at flowering time to promote fruit set.

Thinning Use a pair of scissors to thin out the grapes, starting off by removing the smallest grapes and any that are diseased.

Thinned After thinning, about a third of the grapes should remain on each bunch, leaving space for them to develop.

Harvesting

Grapes require a long season to ripen. Although they may look translucent and feel soft, their sweetness may still not have developed fully. The best test for deciding when they are ready is to pick a few and taste them. If they taste sour, leave them a little longer to ripen fully.

Kiwis

Another climbing fruit plant that is worth growing on the allotment is the kiwi. Do be warned, though—they have lots of luxuriant, rampant growth and will need a sturdy structure to scramble up. Most varieties require both a male and female plant to produce fruit, although modern varieties, such as 'Jenny', are self-pollinating. New plants fruit after three or four years.

Storing & Using

They can be made into: wines...jellies...desserts...salads...

Grapes are best eaten soon after harvesting, though you can keep them refrigerated for a few days. They can even be frozen and make a tasty treat straight from the freezer. Use defrosted grapes in jams and jellies, since the fruit is mushy when defrosted.

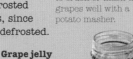

Crushing To make wine, first you need to crush or mash the grapes well with a potato masher.

Homemade wine Making your own wine is an easy and satisfying process; you don't need to buy a lot of specialized equipment.

Grape jelly Grapes are a good choice for making jellies, which are a change from jams.

Harvest Kiwis ripen late in the year and should be harvested before the first frost. They will continue to ripen indoors in the fruit bowl.

kiwi

Melons

Possibly the most delicious of all fruit, this sweet, juicy, tender, climbing annual requires a very warm, sunny site to ripen fully outdoors. Alternatively, they can be grown in polytunnels, cloches, and greenhouses, which allow a wider range of varieties to be tried. Types include honeydew with firm green flesh, cantaloupe with orange-colored flesh, and muskmelon with green-netted skin.

Pollination Melons produce both male and female flowers. Female flowers have a swelling just below the base. To help with pollination, male flowers can be picked and pushed into the female ones so that the pollen transfers across.

Growing

Melons can be bought as young plants or can be easily raised from seed in spring. If growing outdoors, dig over the soil and add plenty of bulky, well-rotted organic matter, such as manure or garden compost.

♦ **HARDEN OFF** plants in a cold frame or porch for a few days before planting outside once the risk of frost has passed. Plant melons 24in (60cm) apart.

♦ **ALTERNATIVELY**, they can also be planted in growing bags with no more than two per bag, or in 12in (30cm) containers.

Melon collar If you fit a collar around the stem, you can water the surrounding soil without wetting the plant, which reduces the risk of diseases.

Sowing seeds

Melons are grown from seed started indoors, since sowing outdoors is too unreliable. Plants intended for growing under cover in a greenhouse or polytunnel should be sown in early spring. Plants for outdoors are sown in mid- to late spring. When selecting varieties, read the back of the seed packet carefully to avoid disappointment—some types won't ripen outdoors. Melons are large plants so don't sow more than you have space for.

Sowing Fill small pots with general-purpose or seed medium, lightly firm it down, and water before sowing four seeds per pot. Cover the seeds with more mix.

Mini-cloche Secure a clear plastic bag over each pot to help retain moisture. Stand the pots in a warm greenhouse or on a bright windowsill indoors.

Growing When they have germinated, grow the seedlings under cover for a few weeks to develop. Thin the seedlings or repot them as required.

Planting outside

Melons are hungry, fast-growing plants, and require rich, moisture-retentive soil to grow well. They also need sturdy supports for their climbing stems, or enough space if allowed to trail across the soil. Melons grow well in containers and growing bags, which can be positioned to provide the best spot, although they will require plenty of water.

Prepare the soil The soil should be thoroughly dug over before planting, adding in plenty of well-rotted organic matter.

Lay weed barrier To help warm the soil, retain moisture, and control weeds, plant outdoor melons through weed barrier.

Clean fruit Planting through plastic prevents the fruit of trailing plants from setting on the soil, keeping them clean.

Routine care

Melons can be left to scramble along the ground but they take up less space when trained vertically, which also keeps the fruit away from many pests. Provide support using stakes and string, and tie in the stems as they grow.

◆ **THIN FRUIT** out when they have reached the size of golf balls to leave about four per plant. Keep them watered and fed.

◆ **FRUIT TRAILING** on the ground should be placed on straw or wood to prevent them from rotting in the damp soil.

◆ **PICK MELONS** when they develop a sweet scent in summer.

Support When growing melons vertically, the fruit also needs to be supported to prevent damaging the stems. Attach strings or pieces of netting to form a sling when the fruit reaches about the size of a baseball.

'Galia'

'Ogen'

Storing & Using

They can be used in: salads...sorbets...smoothies...or can be eaten fresh...

Ripe melons should be stored in the refrigerator, where they will keep uncut for up to 5 days. Once cut, they will keep for 3 days, but should be wrapped to prevent the flesh from becoming dry. Melons can also be sliced or their flesh scooped out into balls, and frozen. The best way to enjoy melon is sliced.

HELP
Troubleshooting guide

Dealing with problems

If you are new to gardening, problems such as pests, diseases, deficiencies, and bolting can sound a little daunting, so it is best to be well informed since there are often steps you can take to keep your crops safe. Monitoring crops closely will help combat any problems that arise, and keeping them in a good, healthy condition will help to prevent them taking hold.

Keeping plants in good health

Remember that prevention is better than cure—keeping plants healthy should help them to fend off many common problems.

- **KEEP PLANTS WEED-FREE** so that they are not competing for nutrients. Hoe between rows regularly to get rid of annual weeds and dig out perennials carefully, removing all the roots.
- **WATER PLANTS REGULARLY** during the growing season and feed them with fertilizers to keep them strong and healthy. This will make them less prone to bolting, see right. Mulch around plants to retain moisture and suppress weeds.
- **PRUNE TREES AND SHRUBS** to remove diseased material and to increase air circulation in the canopy. Remove and destroy rotted or infected leaves or fruit as soon as they appear.

Bolting Some plants, such as spinach and lettuce, are susceptible to bolting, premature flowering that spoils the crop, if sown too early or not watered enough.

Overwatering The roots of crops may rot if they are not allowed to dry out, and this can also cause the fruit to split, especially if the plant is watered irregularly.

Underwatering If you don't water plants regularly enough in the growing season, they will quickly wilt and die. Most plants need daily watering in hot, dry weather.

Cold damage Cold can damage flower buds and shrivel leaves and young shoots, turning them brown. If frost threatens, protect crops with row cover or a cloche.

Natural methods

Nature has its own methods of providing defense but, as a gardener, you can always give your plants a helping hand. Planting wildflowers will attract insects such as ladybugs and lacewings, which will keep down the aphid population; it also encourages hedgehogs, which will help control slugs and snails. Erecting barriers is a simple but effective method of keeping pests from attacking your crops. Fruit cages to prevent bird damage can be purchased, but makeshift ones can be made simply with bamboo stakes and a net. Some pests can be confused by planting other crops nearby. For example, the smell of onions confuses carrot rust flies, reducing the chances of infestation in both parsnips and carrots.

Beneficial wildlife Encourage helpful creatures into the garden by avoiding chemicals where possible, and create inviting habitats using wildflowers and piles of rotting logs.

Insect-proof netting Place fine, insect-proof mesh over plants that are susceptible to damage from butterflies and moths and their larvae, such as cabbage and carrots.

Companion planting Plant flowers near your crops to lure away pests. Marigolds, for example, keep whiteflies off tomatoes, and onions can repel carrot rust flies.

Pests, diseases, and deficiencies

◆ **SOIL PROBLEMS:** If your plant is looking sickly, it is possible that the soil is unsuitable. Check the pH level with a kit (see p.21) to see whether conditions are too alkaline or acidic. Alternatively, check the soil isn't too heavy or light, preventing plants from growing properly. Water and feed plants in sandy soil regularly and improve the soil with organic matter. Plants in clay soil could get waterlogged, so dig in plenty of coarse sand before planting.

◆ **DISEASES:** There are a range of diseases that can affect plants. Look closely to see if there are signs of mold or rotting, and act quickly to remove affected material from your site.

◆ **PESTS:** Larger pests such as birds and rabbits cause obvious damage, but check leaves and young shoots regularly to see if tiny insects are eating your crops. Use barriers to prevent them from infesting your crops to prevent problems later on.

Disguising crops Camouflage your crops in among flowering plants. Not only will this look attractive, but it may help to keep pests at bay.

Gallery of pests

Very few crops are trouble-free, so you'll need to be vigilant and keep a close eye on your developing fruit and vegetables. Be proactive and take simple precautions when plants are young: place a net over trees to prevent bird damage or cover seedlings with row cover or cloches as a barrier to moths and butterflies. If pests do attack, use this gallery to identify them and follow the advice so that you can limit the damage and prevent pests from devouring them.

Wasps These stinging pests go after the sugary flesh on most fruit crops. Hang up wasp traps on trees or place rotting fruit away from the fruit trees to lure them away.

Codling moths The larvae of these pests tunnel into apples and eat their way to the core. Hang pheromone traps in the trees or use an appropriate insecticide.

Carrot rust flies The larvae tunnel into carrots and parsnips, damaging the roots. Surround crops with 24in (60cm) high row cover, and choose resistant varieties.

Leek moths These caterpillars bore into leeks and onions causing them to rot and die. Cover the crops with fabric to prevent the adult moth from landing on them.

Whiteflies These suck the sap from leaves and excrete honeydew. Control includes using an appropriate insecticide or a parasitic wasp called *Encarsia formosa*.

Pea moths Adults lay their eggs on pea flowers in midsummer. They hatch, live inside the pod, and eat the peas. Net summer crops to stop the moths from landing.

Asparagus beetles Both adults and larvae attack foliage and stems of asparagus plants, causing loss of leaves and the stems to die back. Pick off beetles and dispose of them.

Vine weevils The adults eat notches out of the foliage, but the larvae cause most harm by eating the roots, especially on potted crops. Use nematodes as biological control.

Aphids These sap suckers attack and destroy growing shoots and foliage. Rub them off with soapy water, crush them, or use an appropriate insecticide.

Spider mites These cause a bronzed, mottled effect on foliage, particularly inside greenhouses. Use biological controls or a fatty acid to control them.

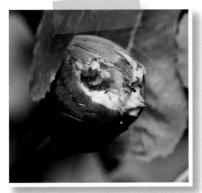

Birds Fruit crops such as figs and cherries can be damaged or completely stripped by birds, which also decimate cabbage and other crops. Protect them using netting.

Slugs These slimy pests attack and devour the stems and foliage of plants, particularly seedlings. Use biological controls, beer traps, or physical barriers to protect crops.

Black bean aphids These sap-sucking aphids attack fava beans, causing distorted stems and foliage. Control by pinching back the top 3in (8cm) of the plant.

Plum leaf-curling aphids These insects cause severe leaf distortion on plum trees in spring. Use a plant oil winter wash to control eggs or an appropriate insecticide.

Caterpillars There are many different types of caterpillars and they mainly feed on leaves and stems. Remove by hand or net crops to prevent adults from landing.

European apple sawflies The larvae damage fruitlets in late spring, causing affected fruits to drop off in summer or scarring larger apples. Remove and destroy infected fruit.

Gallery of diseases

No garden will escape disease completely, so it is important to learn to diagnose the many different types and how to deal with them. Many of them can be avoided by ensuring there is plenty of air circulation around the plants, keeping the roots moist, and removing and destroying any infected material immediately. It is equally important to keep garden tools, pots, and seed flats clean. There are a limited number of fungicides available, so try and prevent fungi, viruses, and bacteria from occurring by practicing good garden hygiene.

Gooseberry mildew The fruits become covered with a whitish fungus. Keep roots moist and choose resistant varieties such as 'Invicta' and 'Rokula'.

Tomato blight This fungus spreads rapidly and causes fruit to rot and brown patches to appear on stems and leaves. Remove the foliage and destroy it.

Downy mildew This disease appears in warm, humid conditions, causing brown patches on the leaves and whitish fungus underneath. Destroy infected material.

Cucumber mosaic virus This virus attacks cucumbers and other crops, causing leaves to appear mottled and stunting growth. Destroy plants and wash tools afterward.

Botrytis Gray mold is often worse in warm, humid weather. Fruit becomes covered in mold and rots. Increase air circulation and destroy infected material.

Canker This causes growths and distortion in existing wounds on tree trunks, eventually resulting in death. Remove infected wood and disinfect tools used.

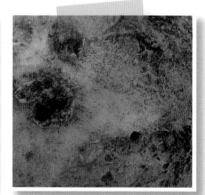

Common potato scab A disease that causes raised brown markings on potato skins. Avoid dry or alkaline soils, lime before planting, and grow resistant varieties.

Chocolate spot This causes brown, chocolate-colored spots on the foliage and pods of fava beans. Remove infected plant material and destroy immediately.

Onion white rot The symptoms are white, rotting bulbs and it can remain in the soil for many years. Practice crop rotation or grow in fresh soil in raised beds.

Potato blight The foliage and stems become brown and eventually wither and die. Remove stems immediately to prevent the infection from destroying the crop.

Clubroot This soilborne disease distorts the roots of cabbage family crops, causing foliage to flop over. Increase the pH by adding lime and improve the drainage.

Blossom end rot This affects tomatoes and bell peppers, causing the ends of the fruit to rot. It is the result of calcium deficiency, so keep plants well watered.

Sclerotinia A fungal disease on lettuce, celery, beans, and other crops. The plants wilt, turn yellow, and fungus appears on the surface. Destroy plants immediately.

Damping off A fungal problem causing young seedlings in the greenhouse to collapse. Increase the air circulation and use clean pots and flats, and tapwater.

Rust This affects many plants, causing orange marks or pustules to appear on foliage and stems. Crop rotation helps, but infected plants should be removed at once.

Brown rot This fungus affects fruit trees, causing the fruit to turn brown and rot. Remove infected crops immediately and increase the air circulation in the canopy.

Honey fungus This attacks fruit trees. Roots develop white fungus and honey-colored toadstools may appear. Remove affected plants and replace the soil.

Powdery mildew A whitish coating appears on leaves and shoots, affecting many fruit and vegetable crops. Try resistant varieties and water regularly.

Silver leaf This attacks plum, cherry, peach, and apricot trees, causing leaves to turn silver and branches to die back. Summer pruning reduces risk of infection.

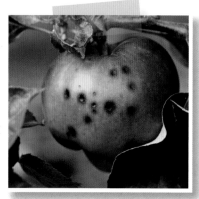

Bitter pit Brownish indentations appear on apple skins, and the flesh tastes bitter. Keep plants watered and mulched; it is caused by drought-induced calcium deficiency.

Raspberrry cane blight This disease causes the canes to become brittle and break easily, and the foliage to wither. Prune to increase air circulation.

Peach leaf curl This affects peaches and nectarines, causing leaves to turn reddish and blister, curl up, and drop off. Keep buds dry in winter with rain covers.

Shothole Brown markings appear on the leaves of cherries or plums, which drop out, leaving holes. It can be caused by bacterial canker or powdery mildew.

Scab Brown angular markings appear on the leaves and fruit of apples and pear trees. Remove infected leaves and fruit on heavy infestations and rake up leaves in the fall.

Scorch Caused by overexposure to the sun or wind, the leaves turn brown and become brittle. Avoid watering at midday and protect greenhouse crops with shade.

Gallery of deficiencies

If your soil is lacking in essential nutrients, plants can become stunted or withered. Although deficiencies can have serious effects on crops, the problem can often be easily remedied by giving plants the missing nutrients.

Nutrients for healthy crops

Plants need a well-balanced diet for healthy growth, but if they are lacking in certain nutrients, they will become sickly. At first glance it may look like a pest or disease problem is affecting your crops. However, if there is no sign of fungus or insect damage, the problem could be due to deficiencies in the soil. A simple fertilizer application is usually all that is required to resolve the situation.

Iron Lack of iron causes leaves to turn yellow between the veins. The edges often turn brown, too. Apply sequestered iron to the soil and mulch with acidic material.

Magnesium This is a common deficiency: the leaves turn yellow and darker patches appear between the veins. Spray diluted epsom salts over the foliage.

Potassium Affected plants have brown crispy leaves and the flowers often do not set fruit. Apply a liquid feed high in potassium, such as a tomato fertilizer.

Nitrogen The foliage turns yellow and the plant stops producing new green shoots. A general-purpose fertilizer and mulch should be applied to remedy the problem.

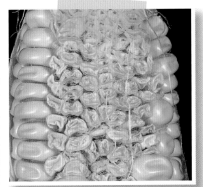

Boron This can cause a range of crops to split, particularly sweet corn, and causes poor root development on root crops. Add borax to the soil or use a foliar feed.

Calcium Lack of calcium can cause blossom end rot or bitter pit, since it affects the plant's uptake of water. Apply lime to the soil and keep plants regularly watered.

Gallery of weeds

A weed is defined as any plant growing where it is not wanted, and in a neighborhood you must be careful not to allow weeds to spread to other people's yards. Digging or hoeing them manually is often a good way to tackle them, and if you don't grow organically, you may choose to use weed killer. As with pests and diseases, prevention is better than cure.

Goosegrass This sticky, clinging weed spreads rapidly through the garden but can easily be removed by pulling it out by hand.

Common problems

Weeds should be removed from around crops because otherwise they will compete for nutrients and water, and they can shade and smother the fruit and vegetables. They also harbor pests.

◆ **PREVENTION:** Cover up bare soil as quickly as possible with weed barrier; otherwise weeds will spread to it. If the soil is going to be bare for a while, consider sowing a green manure that will increase the soil fertility and smother any weeds.

◆ **WEED KILLERS:** If you're fine with using chemicals, weed killers can be ideal for tackling perennial weeds, such as dock and bindweed. Choose a "systemic" treatment, which is absorbed by the weed and will kill the roots. Avoid spraying nearby plants.

◆ **SCORCHING:** This process will burn off the foliage, but it will not kill perennial roots.

◆ **DIGGING:** The most effective method of removing all weeds is to dig them out, root and all.

◆ **HOEING:** This is an effective method of removing annual weeds.

◆ **MULCHING:** Use compost or manure to suppress weeds and stop them from emerging.

Hairy bittercress This small, low-growing annual is a prolific spreader if it produces seed. Hoe it out before it flowers.

Weed-proof fabric Weed barrier can be placed around trees and covered with mulch to prevent weeds.

Dandelion A familiar site in gardens and lawns, it has a deep taproot that must be dug up to prevent its regrowth.

Annual meadow grass This annual grass can rapidly spread and seed all over the yard if not hoed off before it sets seed.

Creeping thistle This perennial thistle is prickly and difficult to get rid of. Either dig it out or use a weed killer.

Shepherd's purse This annual weed produces purple, heart-shaped pods and should be dug up before it sets seed.

Stinging nettle A very common weed that needs digging out thoroughly to remove all the roots, or use a weed killer.

Groundsel This annual produces white seed heads and daisylike flowers. Either hoe or dig it up before it spreads.

Dock This deep-rooted perennial with its large leaves should be dug out completely. Remove all the roots or use a weed killer.

Ragweed This invasive perennial can quickly take over the plot if not kept under control. Dig it out with a fork.

Creeping buttercup Preferring damp soil, this perennial is a persistent weed so the entire root system should be dug out.

Bindweed This climbing perennial is very difficult to eradicate. Consider using weed killer in severe cases.

Pruning

All fruit trees and bushes need pruning if they are to crop well and remain healthy. Although this process can look daunting, there are just a few basic techniques to master. All that is needed is a good pair of pruners, a pruning saw, some loppers, and a bit of confidence to get you started.

Why prune at all?

Most fruit trees and shrubs crop on newer growth, usually between one to three years old. Pruning encourages them to produce strong new stems that will then bear fruit. Pruning trees also removes congested growth in the canopy that would block sunlight from reaching the developing fruit and ripening it. It is also essential for removing dead, damaged, or diseased wood from trees and bushes. If left unpruned, trees and bushes become weaker, producing small, poor-quality crops, and are more prone to diseases. Pruning also keeps plants neat and at a manageable size, preventing them from encroaching on paths or casting excessive shade.

Remove weak growth Thin, spindly stems are unlikely to produce fruit, and just congest the tree canopy, blocking out sunlight and reducing airflow. They should be removed every year.

Tool maintenance

Pruning tools need to be kept sharp and oiled to maintain their performance. Blunt saws and pruners can rip plant growth, leave jagged edges, or cause unnecessary wounds. These can become infected by diseases that can spread throughout the plant, possibly even killing it. Pruning tools should always be cleaned after use, especially when pruning out diseased growth, to keep it from spreading to other plants that are pruned later.

Oiling a saw Before putting saws away after pruning, brush away any sawdust on the blade and wipe it with an oily rag.

Remove rust If rust spots appear on pruners or other tools, remove them using steel wool and a drop of oil.

General pruning tips

Using the correct pruning tool is essential to give clean cuts, and to make the task easier. Pruners are ideal for pruning stems that are no larger than the circumference of a thick pencil. For thicker stems, use a pruning saw. These have long, thin blades that cut cleanly, and are designed to get into tight canopies and cut at difficult angles. Long-handled loppers are also useful for pruning larger branches, although they can cause damage unless they are kept sharp. However, they are perfect for cutting up all the prunings into small pieces. Telescopic loppers are useful for reaching branches higher up.

Branches Use a pruning saw to cut larger branches and get close to the trunk.

Diseased stems Sterilize tools after pruning diseased growth.

New shoots Wispy, new growth can be removed— it will not produce fruit.

Good cut This is a perfect cut, not too close to the growing bud.

Bad cut This rip was caused by blunt pruners that did not cut cleanly.

How to prune fruit trees

Pruning cuts should be made just above a bud. Avoid leaving stubs, which may eventually die back causing infection. However, don't cut right next to the bud either, since this can also cause damage. To make a clean cut with pruners, the sharp, thinner blade should be facing the branch to be retained, and the thicker blade should face the side of the branch to be removed (see above). This avoids crushing the end of the remaining branch. Ideally, the cut should be angled slightly away from the bud. When removing large branches, remove the majority of the weight first to prevent tearing the bark when it is finally removed. Don't make the final cut flush with the trunk, or this can cause dieback. Instead, leave a small protrusion or "collar," which will eventually callous over, preventing any infection from getting in. Try to keep the tree as balanced as possible, ensuring one side is not higher than the other. Remove upright, vigorous shoots, and any that cross or rub.

When to prune fruit trees

Fruit trees should be pruned at specific times of year, either to encourage new growth shortly afterward or to reduce the risk of infection. Trees may also be pruned lightly in summer to remove excess growth or wayward stems.

- Apple and pear trees should be pruned in winter while they are dormant.
- Trees trained as espaliers, cordons, and stepovers (see p.242) should be pruned in late summer.
- Plums, peaches, nectarines, and cherries are pruned in late spring or early summer to avoid silver leaf disease.

Trained fruit trees

Most fruit trees can be trained and pruned over several years into attractive shapes, such as knee-high stepovers, single-stemmed cordons, and elegant fans and espaliers. The purpose of this is usually to save space, and to allow more crops or varieties to be squeezed onto the plot. It can also be to make best use of a warm, south-facing exposure or wall, training the tree to face the sun. Conversely, it can be to reduce the shade cast by the tree, allowing other crops to flourish. Fruit trees can also be trained purely for ornamental reasons, and can create a beautiful and fruitful feature in the yard.

Oblique pear cordons Grown as a single stem with short branches, the trunks of apple and pear trees can be trained at an angle.

Stepovers Apple stepovers need to be grafted onto extremely dwarfing rootstocks. They are ideal for edging vegetable plots.

Fans Cherries, nectarines, and peaches are often grown as fans, usually against a warm wall. Other fruit trees can also be trained in this way and will crop freely.

Espaliers This type of training probably produces the prettiest shape of tree you can grow. Once established, new growth simply needs pruning back to one or two leaves in late summer to keep the plant compact and to retain its shape. Apples and pears are the most suitable fruit trees for espaliers.

Pruning fruit bushes

Fruit bushes and canes should be pruned each year to encourage strong, fruiting growth and to remove any dead, diseased, or damaged stems. Some, like gooseberries, have sharp thorns, so wear gloves as a precaution. Most should be pruned to create a bright, airy, open center.

Summer raspberries Prune summer-fruiting raspberries after they have cropped. Cut out the old canes at the base and tie in new ones.

How to prune

Gooseberries and red and white currants are pruned in summer and winter to produce fruiting buds at the base of new stems, which will then crop the following year. Black currants are pruned at the same time as they are picked by cutting stems that have fruited back to the base. To prune blueberries, remove the lower side branches and cut about a third of the oldest stems to the base in spring.

Fall raspberries Prune all stems to the base in winter. Alternatively, cut some canes down by half, which will fruit slightly earlier.

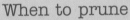

When to prune

Specific soft fruit plants have certain times in the year when they benefit the most from being pruned. Plants such as grapevines, red currants, and gooseberries can be pruned twice a year.

- Grapevines, red currants, gooseberries, black currants, blackberries: main prune in winter.
- Grapevines, gooseberries, red currants: prune in summer, cutting new growth back to five leaves.
- Fall raspberries: winter.
- Summer raspberries: late summer.

Black currants These are pruned in winter by removing a third of the oldest growth at the base of the plant. Use loppers or a pruning saw.

Blueberries Prune these like blackberries, removing about a third of the older wood and retaining younger material.

Red currants These plants also benefit from an extra summer prune, cutting new shoots back to five leaves. Use pruners for this task.

Propagating plants

Most crops can be grown from seed, and although this is ideal for annual vegetables, it is too slow for raising fruit bushes or perennial plants. Instead, to increase your stock, take cuttings or suckers, or divide existing clumps.

Blueberries These shrubs can be propagated by taking 8in-(20cm-) long hardwood cuttings in winter and placing them into a pot filled with acidic potting mix. Take more than one cutting to increase your chances of success.

Fruit cuttings and suckers

Many fruit bushes can be propagated by taking hardwood cuttings in winter. In a sheltered section of the garden, improve a small patch of soil with sharp sand—unless it is already free-draining. Cut 8in- (20cm-) long, healthy, young stems from the fruit bush, and push the bottom two-thirds of each into the gritty soil. Water them during any dry spells, and by next spring they should have rooted, ready to plant out. This technique can be used for red currants, black currants, and gooseberries.

Suckers These are vigorous new shoots that appear from the base of certain plants. They root and grow quickly if potted up and watered well.

♦ BLACKBERRIES and raspberries produce suckers at the base. These can simply be dug up in spring and grown on in pots, until planted out.

Lifting and dividing perennial crops

Once planted, perennial crops stay in the soil for several years, gradually forming large clumps. Over time, these clumps can become congested, and the plant becomes weak. The best way to revive them is to lift the whole plant in spring or fall and split it into sections, replanting only the strongest parts. This often produces lots of healthy new plants, more than you may need, so consider giving any extra ones away.

Herbs Many perennial herbs spread, either creeping across the soil or spreading via underground roots. This makes them easy to lift and divide in spring. Plant the new pieces back into the soil or continue growing them in pots.

Strawberry runners

Strawberries are one of the easiest plants to propagate, since all the work has been done for you. They naturally produce "runners," which are mini plants on long stems. These can be pinned down, where they will take root in just a few weeks.

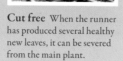

Pin down While the runner is still attached to the parent plant, pin it down into a pot filled with soil mix.

Cut free When the runner has produced several healthy new leaves, it can be severed from the main plant.

Don't be tempted

Sometimes there may seem an obvious way to grow your own plants for free, but there can be good reasons not to do so.

◆ **FRUIT TREES** can be grown from seeds but the resulting trees are unlikely to fruit well, if at all. Buy trees instead.

◆ **POTATO TUBERS** will grow if planted but risk spreading diseases. Buy certified disease-free seed potatoes each spring.

◆ **SUPERMARKET GARLIC** is usually a different variety from what is grown here, and is unlikely to produce a good crop.

Fruit seeds Easy and fun to raise from seeds, fruit trees raised this way will usually disappoint, taking years to even reach flowering size.

Rhubarb This can form a large woody clump in time, which should be divided. Discard the center and split the remainder into new plants with two healthy shoots each.

Asparagus Although this crop takes a long time to establish, mature plants can be lifted and split in fall. Divide clumps into three or four healthy sections.

Globe artichoke These plants can be lifted in winter to reveal small plants called "offsets" at the base. Cut these off, pot them up, and grow them on.

Jerusalem artichoke This large plant is grown for its underground tubers, which, unlike potatoes, can be replanted to grow and produce the following year.

Glossary

Acidic (soil) With a pH value of less than 7, and suitable for acid-loving plants. (See pH.)

Acid-loving (plants and soil) A lime-hating plant that requires a pH of 6.5 or less to grow, or potting mix that has a low pH level and is therefore suitable for growing these plants.

Alkaline (soil) With a pH value of more than 7, and suitable for lime-loving plants. (See pH.)

Annual A plant that completes its life cycle of germinating, flowering, going to seed, and dying in one growing season. (See Perennial.)

Backfill To refill the hole dug when planting a new plant, using soil or potting mix.

Bare-root Plants sold with their roots bare of soil and not in pots.

Beer trap A method of trapping slugs where a container is plunged into the soil and filled with beer; the slug, attracted by the beer, falls in and can't get out.

Blanch 1) To exclude light from growing leaves or stems to make them tender, sweeter-tasting, and pale in color. This is done by pulling soil up around the base of the plants or by placing a pot over them. 2) To plunge vegetables into boiling water for a few minutes, then cool quickly in ice water, dry, and freeze. This helps retain the color, flavor, and texture.

Blet To allow medlar fruits to overripen in order to make them palatable. They are picked from the tree and left in a dark, cool place to soften for several weeks.

Bolt To flower and run to seed prematurely at the expense of leaf or root production. This can sometimes happen to plants because of a change in daylight hours, a sudden cold spell, or a lack of water. Lettuce and spinach crops are prone to bolting.

Brassica A plant in the cabbage family, including rutabagas.

Cabbage collar Circular pieces of cardboard, felt, or other material placed around the bases of brassica plants to prevent female cabbage root flies from laying eggs in the soil surface, near their roots.

Catch crops The growing of quick-maturing crops in the interval between harvesting one main crop and sowing or planting another to make best use of space.

Chelated iron A special fertilizer to help correct and prevent iron deficiency and the yellowing of leaves. It is given to plants requiring acidic conditions, such as blueberries and cranberries.

Chitting To place seed potatoes in a light, airy place, such as on a window ledge, prior to planting. This encourages the tubers to produce small growing shoots, called chits, which grow quickly.

Cloche A temporary structure made from plastic or glass used to warm the soil before planting, encourage early growth, or to protect crops against cold damage.

Countersunk screw A screw that is inserted to sit flush with, or just below, the surface of the surrounding material.

Crop rotation A system by which crops are grown in different areas of a vegetable plot each year, in a three- or four-year cycle. It is used to help prevent the buildup of soilborne pests and diseases that could otherwise occur.

Cure 1) To leave vegetables, such as pumpkins and squash, outside in the sun after harvesting to allow their skins to harden so they will store for longer. 2) To allow concrete to dry out slowly so it sets and hardens without cracking.

Cut-and-come-again A range of leafy greens and vegetables that can be harvested while young, then left to regrow, to harvest again a few weeks later.

Dibber A pointed hand tool, usually wooden, used to create holes in the soil in which to sow seeds or plant bulbs and sets.

Double digging A method of soil cultivation in which the soil is worked to a depth of two "spits," or double the depth of a spade, to create a deep and healthy soil for plants to grow in.

Espalier A tree trained with the main stem vertical and three or four tiers of parallel branches trained out horizontally on either side, supported on a system of wires. Often done with fruit trees.

Evergreen Plants that retain their leaves for more than one growing season; the foliage usually remains green all year.

Firm in To push the soil down firmly around the root ball of a plant immediately after planting, to prevent it from rocking in the wind. Use fingertips to firm in since feet can compact the soil too much.

Fine nozzle (of watering can) A perforated cap fitted to the spout of a watering can, causing the water to come out in a gentle spray. Used for seedlings.

Flower set Flowers that have been successfully pollinated (usually by insects or the wind) and have produced small fruit.

Force To encourage plant growth early, normally by increasing the temperature. Crops such as sea kale and rhubarb can be forced to produce early and tender crops by excluding light. (See Blanch.)

Furrow A shallow, straight trench made in the soil using a hoe or rake, in which to sow seeds. The soil is pushed back over the seeds after sowing.

Germination The changes that take place within a seed as it starts to develop into a plant by sending out shoots and roots.

Graft union A bulge low on the trunk where a tree or shrub has been grafted, or joined artificially; a shoot or bud from one plant is joined to the rootstock of another.

Green manure A fast-maturing leafy crop, such as mustard or heliotrope, that is grown to dig into the soil to enrich it.

Grow on To allow a young plant to develop in its pot before planting it outside.

Hardening off Gradually acclimatizing seedlings that have been started off indoors to colder, outdoor conditions; otherwise they could die from the sudden change in temperature.

Herbaceous A non-woody plant that dies down to the rootstock each year at the end of the growing season, then sprouts again the following spring.

High-potassium fertilizer A fertilizer that is high in potassium (potash). It encourages plants to produce flowers and fruit, rather than leaves. (See Nitrogen.)

Hilling up Drawing soil around the base of a plant to blanch the stems, encourage stem rooting, or to provide support. Potatoes are hilled up to increase the crop and to prevent tubers from turning green in the sunlight.

Interplanting The growing of quick-maturing vegetables between slower growing crops to make maximum use of the space available.

Irrigation A term for watering, or the use of a system of hoses and sprinklers to water plants.

Legume A plant in the pea and bean family.

Mulch A material, often well-rotted manure or garden compost, applied in a layer to the soil surface to suppress weeds and retain moisture. Mulching is carried out in early spring around fruit trees and among rows of vegetables.

Nitrogen A soil nutrient that promotes green, leafy growth.

Offset A young plant that grows from the base of the parent plant; it can be severed and grown on as a new plant.

Overwinter To provide protection for tender plants to survive over the winter period. This may entail placing pots indoors, or digging up tubers, and keeping them in a frost-free place.

Perennial A plant that lives for more than two years (see Annual and Herbaceous.)

pH A measurement used to denote acidity or alkalinity. The scale measures from 1—14; pH7 is neutral, above 7 is alkaline, and below 7 is acidic.

Photosynthesis The process wherein a plant converts sunlight and water into energy.

Pilot hole A small hole drilled prior to a larger hole being made to hold a screw or a wooden post.

Pinching back The removal of a plant's growing tip to encourage bushier, productive growth.

Planting distance The optimal distance for plants to be spaced, depending on their eventual height and spread.

Pollination The process by which pollen is transferred during the reproduction of plants, enabling fertilization and the formation of fruits and seeds.

Pricking out Transferring small seedlings from the seed flat or pot in which they germinated to another where they have more room to grow.

Propagation The production of more plants by seeds, cuttings, division, or other methods.

Propagator A heated tray with a lid that maintains a humid atmosphere and encourages newly sown seeds to germinate quickly.

Puddle planting Planting in a hollow to help retain the moisture after watering.

Raised bed A planting bed that is built higher than the surrounding soil, supported by wooden boards, rocks, bricks, or other material.

Repotting Transferring a plant which has outgrown its existing pot into a larger one.

Root nodule A swelling on the root of a leguminous plant, such a pea, that contains bacteria capable of absorbing nitrogen from the air in the soil.

Rootstock A plant used to provide the root system for a grafted plant. Fruit trees are often grafted onto roots that have been specially developed to control the size of the plant.

Row cover A special lightweight fabric for covering young or tender plants outside when the weather is cold.

Seedling A young plant that emerges after the germination of a seed.

Sow direct To sow seeds straight into the soil, usually into a prepared furrow. (See Furrow.)

Successional sowing Sowing seeds little and often in batches so plants are ready to harvest in succession throughout the growing season.

Systemic Describing a pesticide or fungicide that is absorbed and distributed through a plant when applied to the foliage as a spray.

Taproot The main root of a plant, usually thicker and stronger than the lateral roots, and growing straight downward from the stem.

Thinning out The removal of seedlings, shoots, flowers, and fruit buds to improve the growth and quality of those remaining.

Tilth A fine, crumbly surface layer of soil produced by cultivating it thoroughly before sowing seeds.

Topsoil The upper layer of the soil surface. It is usually fertile and good for growing plants.

Transplanting Moving a plant from one position to another.

Tying in Tying wayward shoots to a support structure, such as bamboo stakes or posts and wires.

Umbel A flower head that consists of a number of short stalks that are equal in length and radiate from the stem, like umbrella ribs. It is characteristic of plants such as carrots, dill, fennel, and parsley.

Verticillium wilt A soilborne fungal disease that results in the yellowing, and eventual browning and death, of foliage, particularly in branches closest to the soil. Remove affected plants and soil close to the roots.

Worm compost An enclosed unit made from stacked compartments in which compostable materials, such as vegetable peelings, coffee grounds, and eggshells, are placed. Special worms turn the waste into compost and liquid fertilizer.

Index

Page numbers in **bold** refer to main entries; page numbers in *italic* refer to illustrations.

Acknowledgments

Picture credits

The publisher would like to thank the following for their kind permission to reproduce their photographs:

Alan Buckingham: 40mc; 43br; 52tl; 53tc; 64mr; 64bl; 70tl; 70ml; 70bl; 72 (all images); 90tc; 90tr; 90ml; 90mr; 90bc; 93bl; 93br; 106-107; 118bcr; 119tr; 130br; 132bl; 136br; 140; 142tr; 148tr; 150; 153mr; 154bc; 156tl; 158bc; 158br; 160tr; 174; 179bcr; 186; 188; 190tr; 191br; 194ml; 195tr; 199tr; 199mr; 202tl; 203bc; 204br; 205tc; 206; 210tr; 211tr; 216tr; 217tr; 218tr; 220tl; 220tr; 221br; 222tr; 222bl; 224br; 226tr; 226bl; 226bc; 226br; 227tl; 227tc; 227tr; 232ml; 232mc; 232mr; 232bl; 232br; 233ml; 233mr; 233bl; 233br; 234tr; 234ml; 235tc; 235br; 236tc; 236tr; 236ml; 236mc; 236bl; 236bc; 237ml; 237mc; 237mr; 240tr; 241tcl; 241tc; 241tcr; 241tr; 242tr; 242br; 244ml; 245tr; 245bcl; 245bcr.

Annabel Akeroyd: 4bl; 7tr; 221tl; Chauney Dunford: 235bc; 236cr; 237bl; Esther Ripley: 230br; Jo Whittingham; 235tl; 235tr; 236br

Dorling Kindersley would like thank:

The growers at Tudor Allotment Association, Park Road, Kingston, for allowing us to photograph their wonderful variety of plots, which helped give this book a rich mix of garden styles.

Boxtrees Nursery Ltd., Walnut Tree Cottage, The Street, Wattisfield, Diss IP22 1NS—for supplying boxwood hedging.

Author's acknowledgment

Firstly, I would like to thank May Corfield for working around the clock to translate and edit my passionate horticultural ramblings into something that sounded great. Thank you also to Alison Gardner for her amazing artistic and creative skills, since she made my words look far better than they deserved. A massive thank you to Alex Storch, too, for being a DIY genius who helped transform my garden from a muddy patch into the envy of all my fellow gardeners. Thank you to Helen Bostock at the RHS for her advice, and also to all the staff at DK, particularly Penny Warren, Alison Donovan, and Chauney Dunford for their support and guidance with the book.

Thank you also to my neighbors at Ranmore Allotments, Dorking, Surrey, and particularly Marina Roberts for her support with this project.

Finally, I would like to thank my beautiful wife, Annabel, and our three children, Guy, Lissie, and Hugh, for all their support during the summer while I wrote this book—and for enduring a rainy two-week holiday in the Lake District while Daddy locked himself away in a dark room and wrote about vegetables.